ENDORSEMENTS

In 2018, Glenn Marsden reached out to my Husband Grant, and I with a bold idea that has since transformed lives and reshaped the mental health landscape. His vision was to create a platform where celebrities and well-known personalities could openly discuss their personal struggles away from the spotlight. What followed was nothing short of incredible. Glenn Marsden is an incredible human being and someone we are proud to call a friend.

His integrity shines through in everything he does, and we are thrilled to support him. Glenn's dedication to sharing his own story is changing lives around the globe, and we are honoured to stand beside him in this journey.

Here's to Glenn Marsden and the remarkable impact of the Imperfectly Perfect Campaign. May it continue to bring light to the darkest corners and remind us all that we are never alone.

CHEZZI DENYER
Executive Producer | Senior TV Producer

Where many of us find our intentions to do good, Glenn finds actions and here is a beautiful example of just one of the many ways Glenn has advocated for mental health awareness and personal growth. The future is in the hands of the present generation who would do well to learn from the past. Reading through the chapters of Glenn's imperfectly perfect life will light a fire inside anyone who's found their intentions and is building up to take action.

A real life regular kid from Yorkshire, who followed his heart and continues to help others do the same, taking his legacy of mental health awareness to the world, even to the epicentre of mental health struggles where many people of Hollywood strive to be understood, it has been so uplifting to see some realism.

This is a real book from a real bloke and it's well worth a real read.

RACHAEL NEWSHAM
Director | Presenter | Speaker | International Health and Fitness Coach

Glenn's unwavering commitment to achieving his goals has led him to a monumental accomplishment: finishing his book! This incredible achievement is something he feels deeply and radiates to all of us. I am immensely proud to be part of the Imperfectly Perfect Campaign—truly, I couldn't be prouder! Glenn has united us all on this empowering journey, creating a blissful moment we can share together.

So, Glenn, I want to extend my heartfelt congratulations on this wonderful book. Congratulations, big time!

IGOR DJENGE
Actor | Producer | Keynote Speaker

In this book, Glenn Marsden is both motivating and inspiring, with a relentless and determined outlook on life. As someone who has witnessed Glenn's unwavering commitment to creating change, I can say his words and journey are a true testament to a greater force driving him. He powerfully demonstrates how personal and spiritual growth can lead to incredible magic and miracles, if you're open and ready to receive them. Glenn shares his deepest wisdom, inspiring readers to believe they too can achieve great success and never give up.

KIM SOMERS EGELSEE
Best Selling Author | TEDx Speaker

Glenn's journey is a powerful reminder of what is possible when we discover our true purpose. His story shows that when we are driven and clear about what we want, nothing can stand in our way. He is a testament of how success is within reach for anyone who is determined, willing to persevere through adversity, and unwavering in their faith. His life is a source of inspiration, offering valuable lessons on the power of resilience, focus, and belief in one's mission."

KRISTI MAGGIO
CEO Maggio Multicultural Academy

ONE MAN'S MISSION TO REDEFINE IMPERFECTION

Copyright © Glenn Marsden

First published in Australia in 2024

by Imperfectly Perfect Campaign Publishing

Lilyfield, NSW 2040

All rights reserved. No part of this book may be used or reproduced by any means, graphic, electronic, or mechanical, including photocopying, recording, taping or by any information storage retrieval system without the written permission of the copyright owner except in the case of brief quotations embodied in critical articles and review.

Because of the dynamic nature of the Internet, any web addresses or links contained in this book may have changed since publication and may no longer be valid. The views expressed in this work are solely those of the author and do not necessarily reflect the views of the publisher and the publisher hereby disclaims any responsibility for them

National Library of Australia Catalogue-in-Publication data:

One Man's Mission to Redefine Imperfection / Glenn Marsden

ISBN: 978-1-7637312-0-2 (Paperback)

ISBN: 978-1-7637312-1-9 (Hardcover)

FOREWORD

'Thank you, Glenn, for the passion, the heart, the sacrifice, and the dedication. It has been a pleasure and an honour to ride with you and do this stuff from day one. Glenn has called me countless times about projects, ideas, and movements, and I have often thought, man, it's just going to take your heart; it's going to take your passion.

You're going to have to be willing to push a pencil up a hill naked. It is all about willingness—how willing are you? Where your willingness ends is where your progress ends, and Glenn has been just so willing to see this thing through.

He's faced people who lie, cheat, steal, and overpromise while underdelivering, all the glitz and glamour thrown at him and the hey's over here along the way. It is a beautiful testament to what it takes to see a something through: the blood, sweat, tears, passion, heart, and dedication.

I am just super proud of you and grateful to be a part of it.'

JEREMY JACKSON
Hollywood Actor | Transformative Breathwork Facilitator | Personal Coach | Meditation Healer

CONTENTS

PROLOGUE	14
A HIGHER CALLING	17
THE MIRRORS HOLD	21
FUELED BY PERSEVERANCE	29
THE REAL PEOPLE BEHIND THE PUBLIC PERSONA	34
A COLLECTIVE STRENGTH	38
ANCHORED IN PURPOSE	41
LIGHTS, CAMERA, PANIC	44
LESSONS LEARNT, BONDS BROKEN	47
HOW DID I FIND MYSELF HERE AGAIN?	52
THRIVING WITH WHAT YOU HAVE	57
SILENCING THE SELF	62
FAITH AND THE AMERICAN DREAM	69
NAVIGATING THE STORM	72
AMERICA, GATEWAY TO ENDLESS POSSIBILITIES	76
ILLUMINATING THE PATH FORWARD	81
NAVIGATING COLLABORATION AND COMPETITION	85
TOUCHED BY THE DIVINE	91
THE END OF A NAIVE HEART	100

WHEN DOUBT CREEPS IN	104
FORTIFYING THE HEART	108
FINDING CLARITY IN THE UNEXPECTED	111
WHEN THE SIGNS ALIGN	113
THE UNENDING SEARCH FOR TRUTH	121
THE MOMENT OF REVELATION	137
THE POWER OF SERENDIPITY	141
REMEMBERING MICHAEL FALZON	146
THE TRUE COST BEHIND FREE RESOURCES	151
SCREW THIS!	155
REDEFINING WHAT COMES NEXT	159
INNER WORK, OUTER STRENGTH	163
IN THE PRESENCE OF THE DIVINE	169
QUESTIONING MY FAITH	177
THE MAN YOU MEET TODAY	183
REDIRECTING INTENTIONS TOWARD IMPACT	188
EPILOGUE	195

DEDICATION

As I embark on this new chapter, it would be impossible to begin without acknowledging the deepest gratitude to the three lights that guide my every step—my wife, Catareeya, and my children, Lincoln and Leighton.

Catareeya, you are the steady anchor amidst the storm, the unwavering strength behind my every decision, and the soft place I land when the world feels heavy. From the moment I began this mission in 2018, a calling placed on my heart, you have stood by my side through the darkest nights and the toughest battles. You have seen me at my lowest, my most vulnerable, yet never once did you waver in your belief in me. Your love is a reminder that even in the midst of struggle, there is always a reason to keep going. You are my greatest champion, my compass when I have felt lost, and without you, none of this would have been possible.

To Lincoln and Leighton, my precious children—you are my greatest purpose. Watching you grow reminds me daily why this mission matters. In your eyes, I see hope, the reason to push forward, and the future I work so tirelessly for. You have sacrificed time with me, yet in return, you've gifted me the understanding of what true legacy means. My heart bursts with pride and love for you both, for your patience and resilience, for the joy you bring into our lives, and for being the constant reminder of why we fight to make this world better.

To every individual who has walked this journey with me, who has shared their stories, their struggles, and their victories—this is for you too. You are the reason this movement exists, and together, we are rewriting the narrative around mental health, one story at a time. Your courage to step forward, to be vulnerable, to join me on this mission is a testament to the power of human connection. Each of you has contributed to changing lives, to breaking down the stigma that has held so many captive for far too long.

I dedicate this book to the voices that have risen to the hands that have reached out, and to the hearts that have found strength in community. You have inspired me, and I am forever grateful for the trust you have placed in me to help share your truth.

Together, we continue to rise, to push boundaries, and to lead with compassion, rewriting the story for generations to come.

Glenn.

THE MIRROR'S LIE

I stand before the mirror's gaze,
A twisted dance in endless maze,
It shows me flaws that others can't see,
But they're all I feel, they're all of me.

I search for answers in the glass,
Each glance, another judgment passed,
My chest and arms, they never fit,
No matter how hard I work or commit.

I chase perfection, lose my way,
In this cruel reflection day by day,
Each rep I lift, each ounce I lose,
Feeds the voice that I can't refuse.

It whispers lies, it shouts them too,
"You're not enough, and they all know it's true."
But others see what I can't find,
A strength, a beauty, of another kind.

But here I stand, no longer chained,
The battle fought, the victory gained,
I've found the peace I sought so long,
The mirror's voice is not so strong.
It showed me scars I couldn't erase,
But now I stand and boldly face,
The truth that rises through the pain—
That worth and love in me remain.
No longer do I seek perfection,
But see myself with true reflection,
I rise above, I stand with grace,
And now, I *embrace my imperfections.*

Glenn Marsden

IMPERFECTLY PERFECT CAMPAIGN

PROLOGUE

"God doesn't call the qualified; He qualifies those He calls."

This saying is like a beacon of hope amid life's storms. It speaks to the idea that divine purpose often chooses unlikely vessels—those who may not possess the conventional qualifications or credentials but are willing to heed the call and allow themselves to be shaped and empowered by a higher power.

Imagine standing at the foot of a towering mountain, feeling utterly unprepared and inadequate for the journey ahead. You might think, "How could I ever conquer such a monumental task?" Yet, divine qualification reveals itself precisely in those moments of doubt and uncertainty. It's as if a guiding hand reaches out from the heavens, offering strength, wisdom, and resilience to overcome the seemingly insurmountable obstacles that lie ahead.

This saying resonates deeply for me, as it reflects the essence of my journey with the Imperfectly Perfect Campaign. When I reflect on the inception of how it all began, I am reminded of the countless moments when I felt ill-equipped to tackle the challenges of mental health advocacy and what lay before me. I did not have all the answers, nor did I possess the network, the skillset, or even the resources that often accompany such endeavours. I was the person standing at the foot of the towering mountain, feeling utterly unprepared and inadequate for the journey ahead of me.

Yet, as I surrendered to the call and looked back over my journey, I discovered that divine guidance was always ever-present, illuminating the path before me and guiding my steps through the darkness. It just took me several years to realise it!

But make no mistake—my journey has been far from easy. There have been moments of despair, questioning, and feeling utterly lost in life's wilderness. There have been sacrifices made, tears shed, and fears confronted. Yet, through it all, I have come to understand even more that there is a flicker of light in our darkest hours, a glimmer of hope that does and will guide us forward if we listen.

So, as I share my truths and lay bare the raw realities of my journey, I do so not to boast of external achievements or accolades but to offer a beacon of hope to those who may be standing at the foot of their own mountains. I want my story to remind anybody that even in our moments of greatest weakness, we are held in the loving embrace of a power greater than ourselves—a power that qualifies, empowers, and transforms us into instruments of grace and compassion.

IMPERFECTLY PERFECT CAMPAIGN

May my journey inspire others to embrace their calling, trust in the process of divine qualification, and step boldly into the unknown, knowing that they are never alone on the journey toward greatness.

ONE MAN'S MISSION TO REDEFINE IMPERFECTION
A HIGHER CALLING

As I pour out these words and reflect on the twists and turns of my journey, let me start by acknowledging something crucial: I am not someone who grew up with religion or spirituality as a guiding force. Hence, I say for many years, I had no idea what I was doing was being 'guided' at all.

As I write my story for you, although I still don't consider myself religious, my journey has led me to a profound realisation—a recognition of the divine presence within each of us. I've come to understand that God's essence isn't confined to the walls of a church or the pages of a holy book but rather resides within the depths of our own being, one that isn't bound by rituals or rules but by a deep sense of reverence and awe for the miracle of existence. It is a journey of discovery that unfolds with each breath, moment of presence, and act of kindness and compassion.

I share this because I want you to know that as you delve into the chapters of my book, I hope you will begin to sense the profound direction my life has taken, even when I was oblivious to it and stumbling in the dark.

IMPERFECTLY PERFECT CAMPAIGN

You may be sitting there right now, reading these lines, and wondering what I am talking about. And that is ok. My journey began with a willingness to listen, to learn, and to absorb the stories of others. I urge you to do the same.

The inception of the Imperfectly Perfect Campaign holds a poignant significance, one born out of tragedy. It traces back to the heartbreaking loss of a friend to suicide. We had not crossed paths for over a decade, separated by oceans and continents. He lived in the UK, and I lived in Australia. Still, the news hit me like a freight train.

With whom I once shared a passion for the gym, this friend had silently succumbed to the darkness that enveloped him. Despite its pitfalls, social media played a pivotal role in connecting me to his story. It was through a cascade of posts mourning his untimely passing that I learned of his fate. There were no warnings, no prior indications of his inner struggles. Just a sudden and irreversible absence, leaving behind shattered dreams and unspoken pain.

And here is where my own story intertwined with his—a tale of my own battles with mental health, (which I will share shortly with you). Turning social media back on after a hiatus, I confronted my own demons, recalling despair I once faced.

His death was a stark reminder of the fragility of life, of the silent battles waged behind carefully curated social media profiles.

ONE MAN'S MISSION TO REDEFINE IMPERFECTION

As I scrolled through his feed, I was met with images of success and happiness—a thriving career, a beautiful home, picturesque vacations, and a loving family. But beneath the surface obviously lay a pain too profound to be captured in a filtered snapshot.

His absence would echo through the milestones of his young son's life, leaving a void no material success could ever fill. Knowing his partner faced the heart-wrenching task of sitting their little boy down, gently explaining that his daddy would never be coming home again.

The weight of those words, the finality of that moment, hung heavy for me in the air, thinking about a moment like that. Knowing his father's absence would be a void that could never be filled. Something which his father's absence would cast a shadow over the milestones of his childhood.

There would be no proud father watching from the sidelines as his son took his first bike ride, no comforting embrace after a scraped knee, and no whispered words of encouragement as he faced the trials and tribulations of growing up. No awkward conversations about crushes and first loves, no shared moments of laughter and camaraderie. Instead, there would be only short distant memories from a young mind that never really knew why his daddy left too early.

IMPERFECTLY PERFECT CAMPAIGN

That realisation shattered me. It forced me to confront the stark reality that his story could have been mine—a husband, a father, torn away by the merciless grip of mental illness.

In that moment of reckoning, I felt sadness, pain, anger, and every emotion possible, but what I also felt was a calling—a whisper from the depths of my soul urging me to do something, anything, to prevent another tragedy like his.

That was the day I felt the call—a call to action, advocacy, and bringing light to the shadows of mental health. It was a call I could not ignore, and it would lead me down a path I never could have imagined toward the creation of the Imperfectly Perfect Campaign.

As I share my journey with you, I hope it ignites a spark of hope within your heart, reminding you that even amidst the darkest moments, there is always a glimmer of light in all of us, guiding us toward our true purpose.

ONE MAN'S MISSION TO REDEFINE IMPERFECTION
THE MIRRORS HOLD

The journey of the Imperfectly Perfect Campaign begins with a searing pain. A pain that tore through me with the devastating loss of a friend to suicide and one because I could not help but confront the haunting realisation, as I mentioned earlier, that my friend's story could have easily been my own.

You see, beneath the veneer of my seemingly idyllic life in Australia—filled with the sun, the ocean, teaching fitness all over Sydney, and the woman of my dreams who went on to become my wife and mother to my first-born, Lincoln—lay a silent struggle, a battle with demons that lurked just beneath the surface.

It began innocuously enough, as a whisper in the recesses of my mind—a whisper that grew louder and more insistent with each passing day as I hit my thirties. It was the insidious voice of Body Dysmorphia, a relentless obsession with my physical appearance that gnawed at my sense of self-worth and threatened to consume me whole.

For me, it manifested in constant checking—obsessing over perceived flaws that only I could see. Picture this: what started as

IMPERFECTLY PERFECT CAMPAIGN

checking my physique for two to three minutes at a time (something most would not think much of) soon spiralled into my worst moments—spending two to three hours standing in front of the mirror, dissecting every inch of my body under unforgiving scrutiny.

I could wake up, ready to take on the day, with a plan to hit the gym. Everything would be set, my bag packed, my goals in mind. But then, I would pass a mirror, and that insidious little voice would whisper, "Just check. See if the results you have been chasing are finally there." Two or three hours later, I would still be standing in the same spot, utterly consumed by the flaws I thought I saw.

The emotional toll was immense — fluctuating between frustration, self-loathing, and exhaustion from battling a distorted image of myself. The mirror became a tool of torment, turning small moments into hours of self-criticism, leaving me emotionally drained and disconnected from the world around me. Despite outward appearances of confidence and competence while teaching fitness across Sydney, I was ensnared in a web of self-doubt and insecurity. Each glance in the mirror behind closed doors became a moment of torment, each reflection a distorted funhouse mirror reflecting my deepest fears. Nobody would have had the slightest idea what I was putting myself through.

ONE MAN'S MISSION TO REDEFINE IMPERFECTION

Teaching fitness, being up on stage, loving everything about what I was doing, yet getting off stage and being alone with my thoughts—it's akin to musicians who, on stage, turn it on, shining under the lights, yet when the crowds go home and they're left alone, who do they have? Nobody but their thoughts. The isolation felt deafening. I recall times working out with friends in the gym, constantly telling them I could not feel the exercises they were giving me working my chest or arms. They would insist on loading heavier weights, but something inside me was already breaking.

Looking back now, I am struck by the irony of it all. I had the physique—the so-called "washboard abs"—and there was nothing inherently wrong with how I looked. But despite all evidence to the contrary, my mind twisted my perception, dragging me into a dark tunnel of self-doubt and insecurity. The insistent gnawing of "check the mirror" grew louder with each passing moment, a relentless whisper that echoed through the corridors of my mind.

Outwardly, I became skilled at concealing that voice, masking my inner turmoil behind a facade of confidence and bravado. To the "boys" around me, I projected an image of strength and invulnerability, unwilling to drop the masculine guard and reveal the silent war waging within. I could not bear the thought of admitting to my mates that I was silently battling demons of insecurity. I feared the stigma and judgment that often-surrounded discussions of mental health, so I kept my pain hidden, smiling on the outside while unravelling on the inside.

Even now, when I look at old photographs, I cannot help but wonder what I was thinking at the time. My physique was everything I had worked for, yet none of it was enough to quiet the obsessive thoughts. The mirror, once a place of fleeting glances, had become my judge, jury, and executioner—pulling me deeper into the abyss of body dysmorphia, all while I kept my struggles hidden from the world.

So, I kept my struggles hidden, buried beneath layers of denial and false bravado. But even as I laughed and joked with my friends, the weight of my inner turmoil bore down upon me like a suffocating blanket. Each glance in the mirror became a battleground, each reflection a reminder of my perceived inadequacies. And yet, I soldiered on, determined to maintain the illusion of strength and stoicism at all costs.

It was not until much later, after the facade had crumbled and the truth had come to light, that I realised the toll my silence had taken on me. The burden of hiding my struggles had only served to deepen my sense of isolation, trapping me in a cycle of shame and self-loathing from which I struggled to break free.

Several months into the birth of my son, Lincoln, with no family in Australia and finding it near impossible to gain full childcare

ONE MAN'S MISSION TO REDEFINE IMPERFECTION

help, my wife and I decided to move to Thailand for a few years to be around her family. Yet as excited about the prospect of me, this English guy, moving to another place of paradise, while intended as a fresh start, it was to be something that only served to exacerbate my inner turmoil.

Making a move, I was cut off from familiar surroundings and support systems; I found myself adrift in a sea of uncertainty, grappling with the relentless onslaught of negative thoughts and emotions that threatened to overwhelm me at every turn. Every day and as the months went on, my despair deepened, the voices grew louder, and the weight of that turmoil became increasingly suffocating. I sought solace even more so in the mirror, a cruel reflection of my inner demons.

Living in the bustling city of Bangkok only magnified my sense of isolation. The vibrant chaos of the streets below was a stark contrast to the solitude I felt high above, in our high-rise apartment. There, alone with my thoughts, the world seemed to close in on me. The constant hum of the city could not drown out the deafening noise in my mind—the relentless barrage of self-criticism, doubt, and negativity.

There were moments when I would stand on the balcony, gazing out over the sprawling skyline, wishing for the storm inside me to calm. I want to be clear—I never contemplated taking my own life.

IMPERFECTLY PERFECT CAMPAIGN

But in those darkest hours, I began to understand how a person could be driven to make irreversible decisions. It was a terrifying realisation—how thin the line is between simply wanting the pain to end and stepping over the edge into something you can never take back. I teetered on that line, walking a tightrope between longing for an escape from the torment and clinging to the faint flicker of hope deep within me.

As my mental state deteriorated, so did my ability to connect with the world around me. I became more isolated, retreating into my own mind. Any excuse to step away became a lifeline for my obsession. Even when we were out as a family, enjoying what should have been precious moments together at restaurants, I would make excuses to rush to the bathroom, where the mirror awaited. I would rip off my shirt and stand there under the harsh lights, tearing myself apart piece by piece, fixating on every imagined flaw.

Even in my professional life, as a business and sales manager at a health and wellbeing facility, the obsession followed me. There were countless times when, instead of focusing on work, I would disappear, jumping on the BTS train, traveling several stops home just to check myself out in the mirror, convinced something had changed in the short time since I last looked.

ONE MAN'S MISSION TO REDEFINE IMPERFECTION

I did not let anyone in. My wife had no idea of the extent of my torment at that time. There was a moment when I even asked her to take photos of me in our home gym—pictures that, when I look at them now, show how incredible my physique really was. I posted them on social media, presenting an image of confidence, of a man thriving in Thailand, living his best life, and in the best shape of his life. But behind that post, behind that carefully curated facade, was a man crumbling. The very same day I uploaded those photos, I found myself back in front of the mirror, silently pulling myself apart once again.

What looked like the pinnacle of physical health on the outside was, in truth, a house of cards—ready to collapse under the weight of my self-loathing. I was trapped in a cycle that felt inescapable, caught between the image I wanted the world to see and the reality I could not escape.

As I sit here, penning these words, my mind drifts back to those moments, and a tear silently rolls down my cheek. It is a tear for the time I missed — time I will never get back. Time I should have spent cherishing my newborn son, being fully present with my wife, embracing the beauty of those fleeting moments. Instead, I was consumed by a battle within, a war no one else could see. The love I should have given to myself—to the person I was and what

IMPERFECTLY PERFECT CAMPAIGN

I brought to this world—was lost beneath the weight of my own self-doubt and torment.

I cannot fully describe the depth of the pain I carried inside. It was not just an ache; it was a hollowness that gnawed at me every day. Even now, as I write this, some of those memories come flooding back, and I shed another tear—not just for the time that slipped away, but for that version of myself who became so lost. Lost in a prison of his own making, where nothing was ever good enough, and the person I was meant to be faded further into the shadows.

I cry for that guy who could not see his worth, who spent countless nights staring into a mirror, tearing himself apart, while the world outside moved on without him. I cry because now I understand how much he missed—the moments of love he could have given, not just to those around him, but to himself. It is a sorrow that still lingers, a reminder of the precious time I wasted fighting a battle I never needed to face alone.

People often say that light shines through the cracks of darkness. For me, that light was my wife. She became my beacon when I thought I was hiding everything so well, but she started noticing my behaviour. She saw what I could not admit to myself.

ONE MAN'S MISSION TO REDEFINE IMPERFECTION
FUELED BY PERSEVERANCE

Before I delve deep here, it is important to understand where I was coming from—a place of loss, a fire within me burning brighter than ever to ensure that nobody else had to endure the pain my friend and I had felt. Like many others, I found myself drawn to various organisations driven to make a difference in the Mental Health Sector in Australia. I was eager to lend a hand, advocate, and even propose the very idea that had been brewing within me—storytelling through visual mediums.

I will tell you, the blow after blow of rejection hit hard, as most organisations either did not respond to me or emailed a polite "no thank you". It was a bitter pill to swallow, fuelled by hurt and determination. There were moments when defiance surged through me, a defiant "I'll show you" attitude. Reflecting on those initial setbacks, I realised that those "no's" were likely due to many other individuals who had faced similar struggles, striving to make a difference and reaching out to these organisations.

At the time, it was difficult to see beyond the rejection. And I will disclose something now. That raw, unfiltered honesty is

IMPERFECTLY PERFECT CAMPAIGN

something you will find throughout this whole book. It is always important to be honest, and in moments like these, we should learn to humble ourselves and recognise that we may, in fact, be wrong. In that, we can gain invaluable lessons in the moments and grow. Come on, we are human, after all.

Looking back, I can now also understand that those hurdles were guiding me towards a different path—a path that, as I was soon to learn, was divinely guided, where I could forge an alternative way and make an impact that was not conformed to conventional ways. Through visual mediums, particularly photography, I sought to connect with people on a deeper level for two reasons with the Imperfectly Perfect Campaign, and I'll tell you why.

1. Photography, Art, Music, and Story-telling all have a universal language that transcends barriers, making them powerful tools for sparking conversations and fostering understanding.
2. I was inspired to take this approach after encountering a national Mental Health Campaign that left me disconnected.

The imagery I was witnessing out there did not resonate, making me realise the importance of creating messages that spoke directly to people's experiences. In my mind, if we were to truly address the stark reality of mental health, we needed to confront it head-on with real, raw, and honest imagery and stories that reflected its true nature.

ONE MAN'S MISSION TO REDEFINE IMPERFECTION

The image in question was part of a national campaign by an organisation some years back. It depicted an old lady clutching a bouquet of flowers. Initially, its message was obscure, but upon closer examination, it revealed that the lady had lost her husband to suicide. To me, it felt disconnected. In a demanding environment, especially in a city like Sydney, where time is scarce and people are constantly on the go, such an image failed to capture attention, especially from our younger generation.

So, in my mind at the time, I was thinking: How many people would this have helped speak up or even draw the correlation between an old lady holding flowers and suicide? Furthermore, I wondered how much money had been spent on a national campaign like this. Let me humble myself here because, for all I know, it may well have done its job. Remember, at the time, there was pain and hurt in me, so in my mind at that moment, it was very much: Are you kidding me? We could not have come up with a better campaign than this? Really?

Now, with what I had in mind for the Imperfectly Perfect Campaign, it was going to be a stark contrast to what I had seen. It would be a campaign that genuinely reflected what mental health looked like from the perspective of those who had experienced it firsthand but from a fresh perspective. I knew that people may very

IMPERFECTLY PERFECT CAMPAIGN

well have argued that depicting the harsh reality of mental struggles would or could be too controversial.

You see, many TV shows have tried repeatedly to drive attention through truths surrounding suicide, but all have come up against criticism. But for me at that moment, the reality was—and do you know what, to this day, still is—that sugar-coating the issue only perpetuates the silence and stigma surrounding mental health struggles. Is that not why, even today, we continue to see the most significant problems being people struggling in silence because, quite simply put… as a society, we do not openly discuss the true reality in public?

Do not get me wrong. Yes, we must be mindful of triggers towards people and sensitive in how we open conversations and deliver them. However, deliberately sugar-coating or hiding the reality through media or programming does not help. Are we, the public, held to place a void over this topic to hide our truths and not come together and help one another? Are we led to believe the masses do not want to hear the truths through a one-sided narrative through a media lens? Perhaps to keep the wheels in motion for public funding to keep researching an area when a simple solution could provide some huge breakthroughs.

Hey, I am not here to make assumptions. I simply share my truths because, for me, the question always remains: how are we

ONE MAN'S MISSION TO REDEFINE IMPERFECTION

ever, as a society, going to start openly discussing these topics and encouraging meaningful conversations to drive positive change if we cannot present discussions in a raw, honest light?

Let us look at the global efforts to address mental health issues and promote well-being. Statistics still reveal a concerning trend: mental health is on the decline, particularly among the younger generation. While we often hear about advancements in mental health awareness and support, the reality usually paints a different picture worldwide. According to data from the World Health Organisation (WHO), depression is the leading cause of disability worldwide among people aged 15 to 19. Moreover, suicide is the second leading cause of death among individuals aged 15 to 29 globally.

These sobering statistics underscore once more what we are often led to believe when we hear about the amount of funding being pumped into the space. The question remains, why is there a disconnection still happening?

IMPERFECTLY PERFECT CAMPAIGN
THE REAL PEOPLE BEHIND THE PUBLIC PERSONA

People often ask me how I started the Imperfectly Perfect Campaign, which had the grand ambition of bringing together the world's most recognised and respected public figures from across every industry to share their stories of vulnerability.

Let me set the scene for you. I am Glenn, an average guy with an audacious goal of connecting with public figures across every industry that people would often pertain to 'have it all' or 'be successful' worldwide to bear their souls. Initially, the idea may sound outlandish, but I did not dwell too much on the logistics. Instead, I dove headfirst into action, using social media to reach out to local public figures in Australia. Sure, I am a photographer, but calling myself a professional might be a stretch. I never had formal training, but I have always been passionate about it. Many often said I had an "eye" for detail. Guess I did, right?

My background was in the fitness industry, so photography came naturally as I often jumped into it as a side hobby, which led

ONE MAN'S MISSION TO REDEFINE IMPERFECTION

me to shoot countless personal trainers. It was not until an actor approached me for headshots once that I realised, I craved something more. Let me be honest here, I got bored very quickly. Just like the standard fitness poses, you can only capture a certain number of headshots. So, I simply asked if the actor would be open to shooting a scene on the spot to capture some raw emotion. Guess it became my calling card.

I used my resources and social media to contact public figures and my camera to photograph them. No elaborate connections or 'secret' knowledge to get introductions made. Just good old social media and messaging. I started by reaching out to public figures from TV shows like Home and Away and Neighbours, as well as to those in theatre, sports, and even the corporate world, where success seemed to have been outwardly attained. Here I was, Glenn, reaching out to public figures who were complete strangers, asking if they had ever experienced their own personal struggles and then asking if they were willing to share those personal stories with myself and the rest of Australia.

You would have thought people would surely have said no. But the responses were overwhelmingly positive, and people started stepping forward. I look back and think how random that must have seemed to somebody in the public eye. A random guy who, let's face it, nobody knew. I was not from an organisation; I had nothing to offer. I merely reached out with a personalised message, often followed up with a voice note, and asked them to share their personal stories and vulnerabilities for a campaign.

Something incredible happened as I continued shooting and sharing these stories on social media. People resonated with the authenticity and vulnerability captured in the images. They saw these public figures not as polished personas but as real individuals with struggles and triumphs like themselves.

It sparked conversations, inspiring others to open up about their own experiences. The impact rippled beyond what I even thought could happen. Colleagues, friends, and even acquaintances were reaching out to the campaign and the public figures who stepped forward, thanking them for helping create a platform where honesty was celebrated. People from all walks of life found solace in knowing they weren't alone in their struggles.

For the public figures involved, speaking out was a monumental bravery. The fear of judgment and potential repercussions on their careers loomed large. Yet, they dared to share their truths, paving the way for others to do the same.

Through their courage, a change began to take root—a shift towards openness and understanding. Each story shared became a beacon of hope, breaking down barriers and challenging perceptions. And I would love to say that when people assume

ONE MAN'S MISSION TO REDEFINE IMPERFECTION

those in the spotlight are merely seeking attention, we have heard and seen it all.

People must grasp the magnitude of those who step forward in the spotlight, sharing their vulnerability and what it truly takes. It is not about seeking further exposure—honestly, they do not need it—it's about them standing up and courageously bearing their souls. The unfiltered them, the imperfect them, the human in a world that often demands perfection.

I will also point out that amidst the bravery, a couple of people stepped forward, later requesting that their images be taken down. When asked for their reasons, both openly said that sharing their struggles on a public forum might affect their chances of booking gigs or hinder their progression with work. This was also backed up by one of the individual's managers. Understandably, their wishes were respected.

Yet, this situation underscores a significant issue. How many lives could their personal stories have impacted had they remained on the campaign as it continued momentum? Yet, they felt their voices had to be silenced due to the fear of judgment or professional repercussions. It is a poignant reminder of individuals' challenges when navigating personal disclosure in professional settings.

IMPERFECTLY PERFECT CAMPAIGN
A COLLECTIVE STRENGTH

My engagement with social media was simple — a means to connect with others. Yet, as I witnessed the detrimental impact of filtered realities on mental health through these social media platforms, especially among the youth, I felt compelled to make a difference.

My mission was clear: to dismantle artificial facades by sharing portraits of the most recognised public figures and hearing their authentic voices, sharing their truths one story at a time.

As the momentum of the campaign surged, so did the calibre of individuals I connected with. Looking back, it was surreal to see how seamlessly doors began to open, revealing pathways to some of the most influential public figures in the Australian professional landscape. What seemed unattainable soon became within reach, as if the universe was orchestrating these encounters. (To which now I know it was.)

At the time, I never stopped to consider the possibility that these connections were part of a greater plan. It all felt so spontaneous, so natural, that I never entertained the idea that there might be

ONE MAN'S MISSION TO REDEFINE IMPERFECTION

something more profound at work. Yet, in hindsight, I now know that a divine hand guided each step of the journey the whole time.

From exchanging words with Rebecca Gibney on her first day in Sydney for an event she was attending, being available for me, to capturing Grant Denyer's raw energy amidst the adrenaline rush of the racetracks I was invited to—each moment was a testament to doors merely opening before me.

Suddenly, the involvement of two of the most prominent and respected public figures in Australia were lending unparalleled credibility to the cause, propelling my efforts to even greater heights. And from that, the floodgates had opened. More of Australia's most respected individuals across many professions were stepping forward to lend their support.

It was as if Rebecca and Grant's endorsement of me and my efforts granted permission for others to speak their own truths, creating a ripple effect across industries that encouraged others to step forward and open up.

Witnessing individuals at the pinnacles of their professions bravely sharing their vulnerabilities was inspiring and humbling. It served as a reminder that authenticity knows no boundaries. Whether you are in the spotlight or behind the scenes, the journey toward truth is universal, and once shared, it can inspire countless people.

IMPERFECTLY PERFECT CAMPAIGN

Suddenly, it was not just individuals who were impacted by this newfound sense of validation. Mainstream media outlets across Australia began to take notice, eager to share my message with the masses. Doors that were once closed now swung open, offering opportunities to amplify my cause and reach even wider audiences.

As articles hit the headlines and networks extended invitations to come on their shows, it became evident that my efforts were making waves. The support of these influential public figures gave credibility to the cause and ignited a national conversation about the importance of authenticity and mental health awareness.

As the movement continued to gain momentum, fuelled by the courage of those who dared to speak their truth, I knew that together, we were making a difference here in Australia, and there was no reason these efforts could not be taken internationally.

ONE MAN'S MISSION TO REDEFINE IMPERFECTION
ANCHORED IN PURPOSE

The first few months of my journey were a whirlwind of joy. Running a gym in the city, spending precious moments with my young family, and making strides in raising awareness for mental health were exhilarating experiences. Witnessing the impact of my efforts was nothing short of exhilarating. Yet, as they say, where there's noticeable change by yourself, there may also be noticeable changes by others with hidden agendas.

I will always remember the introduction to a person working for a company through a mutual acquaintance who was a friend of theirs, with a similar mission to the Imperfectly Perfect Campaign. Their enthusiasm for what I was doing seemed genuine, and the prospect of joining forces appeared promising. At the time, it felt like a match made in heaven – their resources, combined with my passion, could truly make a difference.

However, as time passed, doubts began to surface within me. Intuitive gut feelings, unfamiliar at the time, whispered warnings of discord beneath the surface. Something did not add up. The representative of the company's requests grew increasingly more,

IMPERFECTLY PERFECT CAMPAIGN

veering away from collaboration and toward appropriation. They wanted me to constantly funnel all my efforts and drive attention to them, to provide the assistance people needed because, as they said, they had the actual resources to help people.

Yet, when I often enquired about potential roles within their company, the promises and talk about such things always evaporated somehow and were redirected into 'projects' they could possibly help me with. It never made sense to me. If I were to do all this work to drive attention to them and their marketing efforts through my platform with Australia's most prominent names on board, they would not only benefit from all of my work and already receive substantial funding but also be paid. I said no. I was more than fine driving people toward all the free mental health resources and numbers out there.

The tipping point came when more networks sought to feature my work, and the same representative attempted to insinuate themselves into the spotlight. Their insistence, disguised as a favour for my benefit due to their 'media training,' seemed to finally unveil the companies or representatives' true intentions. I could not have known whose agenda it may have been. Was the representative using their position to power play and look good to those above them, or were those 'above them' in full knowledge of seeing me and what I had created to funnel people to them for free?

ONE MAN'S MISSION TO REDEFINE IMPERFECTION

Either way, it became abundantly clear that my work was being co-opted, not to further a shared mission but to bolster others' own agendas.

Furthermore, when talks of agreements were brought up by myself a number of times, the response I often got was in line with, "Glenn, let's just shake on it because we are both doing things for people to make a difference, right?" Back then, in moments like those, I did find my voice, albeit not the most professional response. Fuelled by a mix of emotions – frustration and a sense of injustice – I spoke my truth. Perhaps my words were sharp, driven by the pain of realising what was happening, which made me constantly believe I was being taken advantage of.

Looking back, I recognise it as a pivotal moment in navigating turbulent waters and for that, I am grateful. I had a choice to succumb to the pressures of feeding others' missions or uphold the vision placed in my heart. It was not easy to make, speaking my truth in frustration at the time, but it was a necessary one. Today, I can look back at that first lesson and understand that whatever the motives of those around me were, this experience was the lesson I needed to learn to stay true to myself and uphold the vision. I am full of gratitude for those involved and for what I went through.

IMPERFECTLY PERFECT CAMPAIGN
LIGHTS, CAMERA, PANIC

Some stories simply beg to be told, if only for their sheer hilarity. Take, for instance, my first appearance on national television. It is a memory etched into my mind with vivid clarity, a tale of nerves, laughter, and unexpected camaraderie.

It all began with an invitation to appear on one of the biggest Sunday morning shows, broadcasting live. This was my first time sharing my work on the Imperfectly Perfect Campaign. To ease my nerves, I invited Marny Kennedy, an Australian actress renowned for her passion and advocacy in mental health awareness, to the show with me. After all, she was one of the biggest supporters and one of the many faces behind the efforts.

As we arrived at the studio, my nerves reached a fever pitch. Sweaty palms and racing thoughts plagued me as we were ushered into hair and makeup. Marny, composed, was chatting away, and laughing with the makeup artists, and I was there thinking, wow, how is she not nervous? I turned to Marny for support in the green room with just minutes to spare before going live. "Help me be less nervous," I recall. To my surprise, she confessed her anxieties about

ONE MAN'S MISSION TO REDEFINE IMPERFECTION

live TV, shattering my illusion of her calm demeanour. Marny reminded me that although she has done TV for years, it has always been pre-recorded shows, so it did not matter if anybody messed up. Live TV is in the now! "Oh, Shit!"

As we took our places on set, surrounded by so many TV monitors and the chatter of the hosts, my nerves only intensified. I felt like a deer caught in headlights, unsure where to look or how to compose myself. From one angle, I could see monitors in front of me with my images from the campaign flashing across the screens and thinking to myself, wow, they looked amazing on TV. At another angle, I could see the teleprompter for the hosts scrolling across the screen. The hosts, ever gracious, attempted to put me at ease with small talk, but honestly, I could feel my heart pounding. Then, the moment arrived – a stagehand signalled our imminent live broadcast. With a countdown echoing, I braced myself for the inevitable. But still thinking, where do I look?

The hosts, the cameras, where? Do you know what? I made it through – albeit with a complexion resembling Casper the Friendly Ghost and eyes darting around like a startled rabbit. Looking back, I cannot help but chuckle at the absurdity of it all. My first time on TV was a comedy of errors, a testament to the unpredictability of live television. But despite the nerves and the inevitable mishaps, it was an experience I will never forget – a reminder to embrace the

IMPERFECTLY PERFECT CAMPAIGN

unexpected and find humour in the chaos. There is a saying that you have to get comfortable in the uncomfortable to grow, right?

Well, my first TV appearance epitomises stepping outside my comfort zone. In those nerve-wracking moments under the glare of the studio lights, I discovered a resilience I did not know I had. It was a baptism by fire, a crash course in facing fear head-on. But despite the palpable nerves and the comical mishaps, I emerged on the other side with a newfound confidence. It was the start of a journey that taught me the importance of embracing discomfort as a catalyst for growth.

ONE MAN'S MISSION TO REDEFINE IMPERFECTION
LESSONS LEARNT; BONDS BROKEN

My journey through turbulent waters was not a one-time ordeal, to say the least. It was a series of experiences, and I have many more to share. Now, I see that they have taught me more invaluable lessons, each one contributing to my growth and resilience. However, one of the most personal lessons came from someone I considered a friend.

Now, I have no animosity or judgment towards anyone. Every interaction, no matter how painful, has helped propel me forward, helping me gain insight and resilience and find my voice. I believe in sharing my story not to cast blame at any time but to offer wisdom that might help others facing similar challenges. One of the fundamental principles guiding my approach is the recognition that people sometimes need to learn the impact of their actions. We are all products of our environment, influenced by the behaviours and norms we observe.

As I mentioned earlier, one experience that hurt me was the pleasure of getting to know someone whom I considered a friend after some time. We shared laughs, trained together, and even

IMPERFECTLY PERFECT CAMPAIGN

worked on projects together. This individual was a staunch supporter of my endeavours, and I cherished our budding friendship. They introduced me to some people who showered praise on my work, talked of grandeur, and helped with my efforts to follow suit. Naively, the intentions of those introductions were genuine. Why wouldn't I?

When another network extended an invitation to feature my work on their show a couple of weeks later, I once more wanted to bring someone along. At that time, I could not think of anyone better than bringing this 'friend' on with me to make me feel more comfortable. Plus, being an avid supporter and helping towards the efforts, I extended the invitation, unaware of how everything was about to unfold. Upon arrival at the network studios, I found myself amidst a whirlwind of what I was told was parallel publicity.

A network executive who had turned up with the friend told the show's host that we were working together. Handing over a tape to the host, the executive emphasised that the friend's new show was closely aligned with the themes of mental health advocacy championed by the Imperfectly Perfect Campaign and to be put into the segment.

Despite feeling out of place, I went along with it, partly because the executive told me not to worry and that this is how everything normally works within media, and partly because I was told they

ONE MAN'S MISSION TO REDEFINE IMPERFECTION

would help my efforts. However, the show passed, and as days passed afterward, I heard from nobody, not even the 'friend.' It was becoming apparent that I had just been used as a pawn to promote somebody else's 'work' by funnelling it through my platform. See a pattern here?

It felt that my actual efforts in making a difference in the lives of others were not being celebrated at all but by companies and people who saw opportunities in my naivety and intentions to further their agendas. A week or so later, I took it upon myself to organise a breakfast meeting I would cover, inviting that 'friend' and the introductions they had made, who raised me praise and said they wanted to help my efforts. The subsequent breakfast meeting arrived, only with the 'friend' showing up with their agent. No, it was not the executive who spoke so much of helping my efforts while seemingly taking over the show, attesting to the 'parallel publicity.'

Nonetheless, it was a person who had also sung praises for my efforts and wanted to 'help' my efforts. I remember sitting there, just hearing conversations about the 'friend's' upcoming trip to Hollywood and watching the plates empty as everybody finished their food. I finally spoke up and asked what the plan was for helping the efforts of the Imperfectly Perfect Campaign. These are the words I will never forget from the agent who had sung praise to me when we first met, saying they wanted to help me: "Glenn, look how far you have come; just keep doing it your way."

I remember not even being mad at that moment. Something in me knew that some people are brought onto our paths filled with empty promises to teach us something. Yet, at the time, a harsh reality check hurt me. Honestly, it wasn't those words that made an impact or hurt; it was that throughout that breakfast meeting, as the 'friend' and I sat across from each other, they remained silent when I spoke, didn't acknowledge me in conversation, and completely avoided eye contact as if I were invisible.

The palpable tension left me questioning my actions and wondering if I had offended or wronged them. Unable to shake off the unease, I reached out afterward, seeking clarification, only to receive a curt reply assuring me that nothing was amiss.

Yet, despite the reassurance, our communication dwindled, and the friendship that once held promise faded into the recesses of memory. It was a poignant reminder of the transient nature of relationships and the unforeseen twists and turns that can lead to their demise. Reflecting on the situation, after so long of trying to determine if I had done something wrong, I concluded that I did not even need to know the exact reasons behind the friend's withdrawal.

ONE MAN'S MISSION TO REDEFINE IMPERFECTION

What truly mattered was accepting that the experience, like many others that would soon play out in my life, was part of the ebb and flow of my journey. This experience was a painful lesson that led once more to personal growth and taught me resilience. An experience like many more to share with you all that I hold no resentment towards.

IMPERFECTLY PERFECT CAMPAIGN
HOW DID I FIND MYSELF HERE AGAIN?

Moving away from my fitness career and stepping into construction as a labourer, working six to seven days a week, twelve hour days, on alternate shifts, day, and night, I wondered where all of this was going. You see, throughout my career choices, I was the guy who raised his voice when something was not right, especially for those who would not speak up for themselves.

I have always been guided by morality but found it detrimental when speaking up, too. So, how did I end up in construction?

The simple answer is that I stood up for myself and a colleague in my position within the Fitness Industry, and it was the straw that finally broke the camel's back, as the saying goes for me. During the first half of starting the Imperfectly Perfect Campaign, I worked in management for a health club in Sydney. Despite initially great beginnings, it became different. There were too many cooks in the kitchen, and the micro-management was suffocating.

ONE MAN'S MISSION TO REDEFINE IMPERFECTION

As club managers, we were told we had to have lunch at our desks, we could not leave the club during breaks and we could not clock out until one minute past finishing time. It was ridiculous, and it was clear there were no legalities in place, or the owners thought they could treat people this way.

That was until they met me, who often spoke up about these rules they had in place. It reached the point where I had been there for over six months and had used my lunch breaks to do precisely what I wanted, leave the facility to get food or check my personal emails, as had my colleague.

This was not seen in a good light by head management. I received an email regarding a performance meeting to go to the head office. As serendipity would have it, that same day, something happened that changed everything. Two construction workers came to train in the gym. I started talking to them, and something in me just wanted to ask about the city projects they were working on, whether it was hard to get positions on them, and whether the pay was worth it. It took one conversation, a phone call to book several courses to attain a white card to work in construction, and an exchange of details with the guys, and I had made my mind up.

I sent a quick email to the club management stating some legalities around 'rules' for employees and linking them to employee rights. They wanted me in for a 'performance review,' so

IMPERFECTLY PERFECT CAMPAIGN

I followed up with a short email with an attachment of my notice. The following week, I attained my white cards, and the two men I spoke to at the gym followed through and lined me up for an on-site position with them. See how it all seemed to fall into place. But I often pondered, how did I end up here again? I can look back at many experiences of speaking up for things I saw were not right.

Let me take you back to my time back home in the UK. I worked in hospitality during and after college, where I had given several years to a particular establishment. During the Christmas period, a new manager who had recently joined the establishment told me during a 14-hour shift that I and the rest of the waiting staff would have to clock off after the shift and be back for the breakfast shift, giving us only four hours of sleep. The women were tired and in tears; the guys were frustrated. What did I do? I stepped forward and spoke up!

Guess what? Glenn was told that he could leave early.

The next day, I was asked to go to the office to see this 'new' manager and told that they were letting me go. The irony was that, firstly, given how long I had worked there, it was a case for unfair dismissal, which they should have very well known. Secondly, the same day, I walked straight into the fitness centre next door to the establishment. I went and sat in the pool, frustrated, and one of the hotel owners I knew was in the pool simultaneously. He asked why

ONE MAN'S MISSION TO REDEFINE IMPERFECTION

I was not at work. That is how long I had worked at the establishment and had known the owners very well. I told him what had happened, and his anger said it all. I recall him getting straight out of the pool, saying he would get it sorted immediately, and wanting to know who had let me go.

Relationships are a strong forte of mine, and I had given several years to this establishment and knew the owners very well. So, part of me knew that when he told me he would sort it immediately, somebody was about to get their servings quickly.

Now, heading out of the pool and sitting at the gym cafe, I also mentioned it to the gym staff I had got to know, and unexpectedly, I got offered a job on the spot. Funnily enough, I got called the same evening by the 'new' manager from the establishment who let me go, sheepishly calling to tell me they had made a mistake. Little to say, I did not go back to the establishment.

Being let go from speaking up led me to my career in the Fitness Industry, which spanned over 20 years and took me internationally. My point here is that my morality and integrity have always been within me. I never realised at those times how important they would become in shaping me for what was placed on my heart to bring out to the world with the Imperfectly Perfect Campaign.

Speaking up for change and having morals set me in good stead for what would come. Although I used to get frustrated and wonder

IMPERFECTLY PERFECT CAMPAIGN

why it was happening to me, the reality was that everything was happening FOR me—a push to move to the next step of my journey. Did you notice how a 'serendipitous' moment had stepped in again?

ONE MAN'S MISSION TO REDEFINE IMPERFECTION
THRIVING WITH WHAT YOU HAVE

As the months continued and I settled into the rhythm of working alternate days and nights in construction for twelve gruelling hours, I was blown away by how I got through everything to make anything move. Here I was, a guy with no prior experience, no resources to speak of, just a burning mission to change the narrative around mental health. Armed with nothing but my camera and the support of willing celebrities and public figures, I knew I had to start thinking about how to get this message further out into the world.

Luckily, with the help of the public figures and the media attention the Imperfectly Perfect Campaign gained, the marketing and messaging took care of itself within Australia.

Now, you might think that sounds great, and in many ways, it was. Articles were popping up across multiple mainstream publications, the biggest names in Australia featured my work, and the momentum of making an impact was growing daily – a massive accomplishment. But behind the scenes, you must remember there was just one guy – me.

IMPERFECTLY PERFECT CAMPAIGN

Many people were reaching out, pouring their stories to me, wanting to come on board. Yet, I was trying to navigate everything. I certainly could not expand my bandwidth. I was there, learning about networking, trying to understand facets of marketing, wrapping my head around social media accounts, learning how to set up a website, and even trying to figure out how to build a database to keep people informed. And then obviously, there was organising the photoshoots with the public figures, followed by the production afterwards – it was overwhelming, to say the least.

Let me walk you through a typical day back then.

4 am – gym time, my moment to keep my fitness up while listening to podcasts to absorb knowledge about everything I needed to learn.

By 6 am, I would be on the construction site, gearing up for another 12-hour shift.

By 6 pm, I would clock off and hop on the bus to get home by around 6:45 pm. I would have a quick dinner and snatch an hour with my family before they turned in for the night.

Most nights, from 8:30 pm to midnight, I built the website, researched marketing strategies, learned public relations, crafted pitch decks, and figured out how to find help.

This was my life, solidly, for months on end. Eventually, I had everything running like clockwork. It sounds almost comical, but I

ONE MAN'S MISSION TO REDEFINE IMPERFECTION

became a master at posting, reaching out to networks, managing multiple social platforms, and understanding how to leverage a message for maximum impact. I even became resourceful at building community databases without money.

I was utilising platforms that allowed two thousand contacts for free and had several accounts to keep everybody interested in finding out more about the efforts and being a part of the community updated. Want to know how hard that is!

At this point, I must credit two incredible women, Karen Ledbury and Jacinta Tynan, who not only supported the Imperfectly Perfect Campaign but also provided valuable assistance in the realm of media and public relations. They helped me navigate the unfamiliar waters when I was trying to craft press releases and understand how the media machine worked.

Remember that I had been seemingly 'used' not once but twice to drive attention through my work to others? Well, it had obviously left me with a profound sense of caution. If I was going to discern when people or companies were attempting to exploit my efforts, I needed to understand how everything worked. So, it was essential to seek insights and help from those who had a thorough understanding of media dynamics. This enabled me to distinguish genuine opportunities from potential pitfalls. These ladies were an amazing help.

IMPERFECTLY PERFECT CAMPAIGN

Now, that is not to say I saw all the pitfalls ahead. Because, well, I did not. And a pitfall that was to shortly follow that I had not seen coming really dove into how scrupulous certain publications can be in driving a narrative to something that simply causes controversy. I will elaborate on this experience shortly.

Despite not having any funds for the campaign and investing everything I was earning towards getting everything up and running, the rapid growth and attention from external sources led to questions about whether my initiative was a charity or a non-profit organisation. In truth, it was a passion project that had gained so much traction that it outpaced my ability to keep up with all the questions around me.

Imagine this: I was finally getting everything running smoothly, still juggling twelve hour shifts in construction while also trying to figure out various aspects of the campaign, nonetheless enjoying it all. On top of that, it was as if I had to now decide what to do and say about the Imperfectly Perfect Campaign because everyone wanted to know. I vividly recall being on the first TV show with Marny, and mind you, within only three months of the campaign starting, at one point, the host asked,

"So now that you've done this, what's next?"

ONE MAN'S MISSION TO REDEFINE IMPERFECTION

In my head, I was thinking,

"It's only just begun, what do you mean."

It could have been so easy to get lost in the noise, with everyone else's opinions and expectations clamouring for attention. Still, in the beginning, I just seriously had to try and stay focused to keep pushing forward. Fuelled by the passion and remembering the why in me, that ignited this mission placed on my heart in the first place.

That is not to say that after some time of people constantly searching for answers about the Imperfectly Perfect Campaign, it did not become overwhelming because, simply put, it did for me. At one point, I succumbed to the pressure to seek advice from everyone who was telling me what it should be.

IMPERFECTLY PERFECT CAMPAIGN
SILENCING THE SELF

With so many voices becoming louder than my own, there came a period where I began to seriously silence myself. The world around the Imperfectly Perfect Campaign was expanding, drawing attention from all angles, and like I had mentioned, the questions were all around me:

What are you going to do with it?

What is it?

Are you a charity?

What are your plans, Glenn?

It is a profound observation, though, isn't it? The innate human curiosity to understand the purpose and direction behind something, even when the present moment holds its own significance. It speaks volumes about our societal conditioning, the constant pursuit of meaning and understanding, and having to know.

There is a prevailing belief that every action must serve a purpose or lead toward a specific end goal. As a result, we incessantly seek answers to questions about why and what

ONE MAN'S MISSION TO REDEFINE IMPERFECTION

something is working towards. On reflection, this point in my journey really does serve as a reminder to anybody reading this that whilst we always feel that we 'have to know,' we risk overlooking the beauty and significance of the present moment and what is happening or being achieved.

We overlook our actions' impact in the here and now, the joy and fulfillment they bring, and the help they bring to others independent of any future outcomes. Perhaps it reflects our collective need for control and certainty in an uncertain world. By understanding the purpose and direction behind something, we attempt to gain a sense of security and stability, even if it is illusory.

Amidst this relentless pursuit of answers, we sometimes forget to appreciate the journey, the moments of joy, connection, and growth that unfold along the way. We forget to be grateful for what is happening now, for the simple fact that we are alive and experiencing life in all its richness and complexity.

So, while the questions may persist and the need for knowing may remain, it is worth pausing to embrace the present moment. To revel in the beauty of what is happening now, the difference something is making in that moment, and the gratitude for simply being here, experiencing life in all its glory.

Anyway, back to the story.

IMPERFECTLY PERFECT CAMPAIGN

As though I was not doing enough, I delved into the 'professional' platform (as they call it) of LinkedIn through various networking groups to connect with people and seek advice in non-profits, charities, anything really. I did not honestly know where to start. I mean, you start a passion project that outwardly gains traction quickly. Then what?

It is not exactly as if you have all the answers, know where people in these areas hang out, or have them on speed dial to ask. Well, I did not have all the answers anyway. So, getting into LinkedIn and coming across so many 'professional' networking events, I will be honest with you. I could just never truly connect with them.

It felt akin to stepping into a scene from the TV series Dragons' Den or Shark Tank. In so many of these networking events, attended by anywhere from twenty to fifty individuals, the facilitator always pushed for a one to three-minute pitch. To me, it begged the question: Is this really networking?

Amidst the flurry of pitches, I struggled to recall what the first person said, let alone the tenth. Moreover, I did not see myself as there to sell; I was there to genuinely connect and network. Frustrated by the need for meaningful connections, I took it upon myself to create my own networking events, despite not knowing many people.

ONE MAN'S MISSION TO REDEFINE IMPERFECTION

I have no idea where I got this ability to put into my head that if you are not invited to the table, you make your own. If you do not connect in places, you build your own places and bring your own people to them. Drawing from my background in bringing people together through fitness, I merely posted invitations on the platform, and to my surprise, they started to gain traction.

Through these events, I had the opportunity to meet some truly incredible individuals. However, navigating LinkedIn proved to be a mixed experience, and I want to share this here because many people can benefit from what I learned. While many touted it as a professional platform, I soon discovered that it also harboured individuals seeking to take advantage of others just like so many other platforms, that you see it.

I say here to anybody seeking or looking to network: Please always have your bearings and do your due diligence. Nevertheless, as I mentioned, I also met some incredible people amidst the noise and the rest of it. I received advice about transitioning towards a non-profit structure, which I had been seeking. One pivotal moment came when I spoke with a lawyer who became involved in my networking events.

Their invaluable advice shed light on the complexities of non-profit regulations and requirements, presenting new challenges that I had not anticipated because, quite frankly, I had no clue about them. Suddenly, it would not have been about maintaining momentum anymore; I would suddenly have to weigh the legal and financial implications of every decision to do a non-profit. Each choice would feel like a test, demanding careful consideration and strategic planning. I would have had to navigate this unfamiliar terrain all alone, and honestly, a non-profit was not even on my radar at any point until I started allowing myself to be drowned out by all the noise and listening to everybody else.

For me, I was simply doing myself. I was immersed in the flow of pursuing my passion, fuelled by creativity and a desire to serve others, and opportunities seemed to effortlessly unfold before me. As the weeks continued, I connected with more remarkable individuals who shared their insights about non-profits, and this is where things slightly changed in my mind, for a hot moment at least. As I mentioned, it was not even on my radar, but I seriously contemplated starting one.

Now armed with several people being put before me and interested in helping, this may be the next step. I mean, I would no longer be alone. So, I finally submitted, and with the encouragement and support of getting to know several incredible people who wanted to help, plans were set in motion over the next couple of months to bring on a board of directors and proceed with establishing a non-profit.

ONE MAN'S MISSION TO REDEFINE IMPERFECTION

However, as we drew closer to finalising paperwork and formally appointing the board of directors, I could not shake the feeling that:

a) Things were moving too fast.

b) For some reason, despite my inability to articulate it then, my intuition told me that this was not aligned with my true purpose and that I should not pursue it.

In a moment of clarity, I decided to halt the process the evening before we were scheduled to sign the paperwork. I emailed everyone involved, expressing my gratitude for their passion and support but explaining that I needed to pause and reassess. To my relief, they were understanding and supportive.

In hindsight, looking back on my decision to pursue a non-profit and everything it would entail, it weighed heavily on my mind constantly. It was during this time that the campaign experienced a standstill. Despite my continuous efforts to network and reach out to others through this period, there was a palpable disconnection, and I could not understand why.

Everything had been just gaining momentum from all angles, and suddenly, NOTHING. Yet, looking back, I realised that by releasing the pressure to conform to external expectations and listening to that 'nudge'—the intuition that a non-profit was not

IMPERFECTLY PERFECT CAMPAIGN

meant to be—I had created space in my energy field, allowing new opportunities to emerge.

Indeed, as soon as I consciously decided to follow my intuition and forego the non-profit route, the floodgates opened again. Not only did opportunities continue to flourish in Australia, but America also extended a beckoning call. So here is a powerful reminder to anybody reading this: the importance of trusting your inner voice and remaining true to your authentic path, even in the face of uncertainty and external noise. That inner voice, that intuitive nudge you feel, is NEVER WRONG!

ONE MAN'S MISSION TO REDEFINE IMPERFECTION
FAITH AND THE AMERICAN DREAM

As America beckoned and a surge of energy propelled me forward, though the initial intuition I had previously felt that something wasn't meant to be with starting a non-profit, it was as if it had turned on its head this time and had awakened a sense of intuitive excitement in my stomach constantly, with the possibility to the opportunity to take my efforts genuinely global.

Despite the excitement, the apparent task was: how would it happen? Lacking resources and facing the daunting task of financing the journey myself (which, quite frankly, I did not have), I just felt this knowing it would happen. Do not ask me how! Amidst these deliberations, the suggestion of launching a GoFundMe campaign arose from the individuals I had connected with during discussions about the potential non-profit venture.

Yet, despite our hopes and the traction of the campaign's efforts, the response was modest, with only a handful of generous souls contributing to our cause. Again, it is something I look back on now and see that it was never meant to be. You see, I never felt that I wanted to take the efforts towards a place of asking for donations.

IMPERFECTLY PERFECT CAMPAIGN

I always saw myself, and I had never told anybody this, as a bit of a Robin Hood figure who wanted to take from the rich (the companies that could afford things) and give to the poor (those who needed help). At the time, with all the noise as I had been saying, I listened to everybody around me. They all had great intent in helping, so we tried, but clearly, it was never meant to be.

In a moment of thinking, "Well, maybe it's not meant to be," I found myself instinctively turning to a higher power, silently imploring for guidance. Weeks passed, and it seemed as though my dream of travelling to America to take this mission global was slipping out of reach.

Then, out of nowhere, a serendipitous phone call with a friend from the USA sparked a chain of events that would alter the course of my journey. Upon learning of some of my photography was used without permission, I was advised to seek compensation.

Naive and unsure of how to proceed, I turned to the counsel of one of the incredible women who had guided me through the complexities of the potential non-profit endeavour. Within two weeks, I received an unexpected remuneration from the company that used my work, which would cover the costs to the USA. It truly was a miraculous turn of events that I never saw coming.

And as I reflected on the remarkable turn of events, it became undeniably clear that a higher force guided my journey with

ONE MAN'S MISSION TO REDEFINE IMPERFECTION

unparalleled precision. Those intuitive nudges to refrain from starting a non-profit organisation rang true, for as soon as I pulled away, America extended its welcoming embrace. While the attempt to garner support through a GoFundMe campaign did not yield the desired outcome, divine intervention manifested in unexpected ways. Instead of relying on external contributions, the necessary funds materialised through the fruits of my labour outside the Imperfectly Perfect Campaign.

It was a humbling realisation that the universe was conspiring in my favour, orchestrating a path forward that defied conventional logic. All I needed to do was trust and know the universe was conspiring for me. In trusting and relinquishing control over the outcome, just having a knowing (that I had no clue where it came from), I allowed space for miracles to unfold, demonstrating the profound power of divine guidance in shaping our destinies.

IMPERFECTLY PERFECT CAMPAIGN
NAVIGATING THE STORM

I once heard the saying, "Are you ready?"

It is a question that applies not only to achieving our goals but also prompts us to consider whether we are prepared for the unforeseen challenges that may accompany success.

Are we ready for the influx of money, fame, or attention, and how will we respond when faced with criticism or adversity?

As I embarked on the journey of bringing the Imperfectly Perfect Campaign to America, amidst my daily grind in construction, unexpected lessons in resilience awaited me.

One such lesson unfolded with the publication of an article highlighting the campaign and the public figures involved.

One of Australia's most prominent public figures, renowned for their public relations and marketing career, had recently lent their support to the cause. Their openness about their own struggles and the pitfalls of media portrayal resonated deeply.

However, when the article was released, it was not the positive response we had hoped for or that we had been constantly receiving about our efforts in trying to make a difference.

ONE MAN'S MISSION TO REDEFINE IMPERFECTION

The headline featured the very person who had supported us, yet the comments section was filled with vitriol and scepticism. Words like "insincere" and "disservice" stung, and the onslaught of negativity from people, especially towards the person in question who had stepped forward and shared their story, was vile.

I always remember one comment that stuck out regarding the campaign's efforts, leaving me questioning the validity of my efforts. It was baseless to suggest that I should direct all my efforts towards the larger organisations already out there.

I felt compelled to defend everything against these baseless attacks. In my frustration, I spoke to the public figure who the article had led with. Their response was a revelation. They reminded me that criticism and scepticism come with the territory of putting oneself out there. They likened it to water off a duck's back, advising me to focus on my mission, thinking of why I started it and who I was trying to help. Most importantly, they advised me to drown out the noise because some people would always be making it.

It was later, that I was also made aware, which was unbeknownst to me initially, that the publication was known in the Public Relations and Marketing sector. So, these were not comments coming from the public I was trying to help, but baseless negativity from people who would have had a problem with the person in question, thus a problem with who or whatever they were working on or connected with.

It was another pivotal moment of realisation. I had to learn to differentiate between constructive criticism and baseless negativity, to stay true to my purpose despite the detractors.

In a world where competitors are quick to cast judgment, it is imperative to challenge the notion of infallibility and advocate for empathy and understanding. Too often, people are judged based on past actions or industry affiliations without consideration for personal growth or the complexities of individual experiences.

Yet, behind every facade lies a story of struggle, trauma, grief, and mental health challenges—universal human experiences that transcend profession or status.

It is a lesson in humility and compassion, a call to recognise the inherent flaws within us and others, and to refrain from casting stones in glass houses. Instead of rushing to judgment, we must strive to understand the journey that has shaped each individual, acknowledging the potential for growth and transformation.

By fostering a culture of empathy and acceptance, we pave the way for genuine connection and healing. We create space for forgiveness and redemption, allowing individuals to transcend their past and embrace a future defined by possibility and potential.

ONE MAN'S MISSION TO REDEFINE IMPERFECTION

It was this experience that truly cemented a deeper meaning for me in my mission of the Imperfectly Perfect Campaign, to help others realise the profound understanding that imperfection is not a flaw to be condemned but a shared human experience to be embraced.

And in advocating for acceptance and understanding, we can all break free from the constraints of judgment and truly help one another.

Finally, to anybody implying the necessity of me directing everything towards larger organisations, my response became straightforward:

"Why would I do that?"

It is akin to suggesting to anyone, "Why bother starting your own business or service when there are already established corporations offering the same products or services?"

Why not simply defer to them or funnel everyone towards them?

The truth is, people are driven to start their own ventures or missions because they perceive a gap, a disconnect in what is currently available or out there.

It is not to judge, condemn, or say it is wrong, but like anything in this world, to make a change, things require change.

Things demand breakthroughs from fresh ideas to potentially alter the course of the world.

IMPERFECTLY PERFECT CAMPAIGN
AMERICA, GATEWAY TO ENDLESS POSSIBILITIES

Armed with a mix of excitement and apprehension, my arrival in America unfolded without much planning. Reflecting on it now, I find it amusing how America suddenly started beckoning me with an intuitive pull and excitement towards it, yet it was without me fully comprehending why.

Other than the country suddenly gaining interest in my work from various publications and networks wanting to interview me and share my endeavours, I had not really got a 'game plan' as such, to know exactly what I was supposed to do other than these interviews. I just knew I had to be there and knew something was about to happen for me and my efforts.

The trip became noticeably clear extremely fast that it was America that held the potential to amplify my efforts on a global scale. Armed with my camera and a couch to crash on at a friends, that is all there was of me.

ONE MAN'S MISSION TO REDEFINE IMPERFECTION

On my first day, I not only coordinated the interviews I had lined up with interest in the Imperfectly Perfect Campaign but also started thinking about connecting with people.

How does Glenn do that?

Hitting the nearest gym.

Now, people always ask, why the gym?

Well, do not get me wrong, I love the gym first and foremost, but it is also a place I connect, I network, and I get to form solid connections with people based on their true selves very easily.

I mean, let's face it. With a career spanning over twenty years in fitness, I can talk to anybody, and I do. People at the gym do not walk around with their 'professional attire' on. They do not flaunt what they do for a living, and egos are left at the door. For me, they always create a sense of community where you truly get to know the real people there.

So that is what I did. I joined Gold's Gym while in Venice and started getting to know people almost immediately each morning.

Then, I would spend my first few afternoons reaching out to public figures who I found were openly speaking about mental health, just as I had done in Australia. Hey, if it worked in Australia, why wouldn't it anywhere else?

What had I to lose, right?

IMPERFECTLY PERFECT CAMPAIGN

I had no trepidations about what would happen if I did not hear from people. I just acted with conscious thought.

It was not until the third day that I recall heading on Instagram and getting ready to reach out to more public figures. But what came across me immediately, as I opened the app, was a post by Jeremy Jackson (former Baywatch star, the show watched by over nine billion viewers weekly around the world).

It was strange. I was not following him on social media, even though I had grown up, like many people, watching the show. I did not know, see, or follow what the cast of Baywatch were up to all these years later. Nevertheless, a random post popped up on my feed when I opened Instagram.

Obviously, I saw his name and recognised it, but all these years later, he isn't that kid we saw running on the beach with David Hasselhoff, is he?

Regardless, the post must have been profound to me at the time because something told me to reach out to him at that moment.

Here I am in Los Angeles, with my phone in hand, thinking, "Okay, let's do this." And do you know what? That very same evening, I received a message back from Jeremy. So, I sent a voice note to him.

ONE MAN'S MISSION TO REDEFINE IMPERFECTION

People laugh when I say I have sent voice notes to every person who has supported the efforts. First, I would reach out by message, and then, if and when I hear back, a voice note would follow.

I have always wanted people to hear from me, hear the sincerity in my voice, and understand why this is so important to me, and that has never changed. I am the guy who sends voice notes!

Anyway, I explained to him what I was trying to do and asked if he would be keen to do a photoshoot while I was in town. Jeremy let me know that photoshoots were not really his thing.

Growing up on a show where it was all about how you looked, he had moved away from wanting to be doing more shoots, but he said something to me: "There is something about you, Glenn, so yes, I will."

We arranged to catch up a couple of days later in Culver City. What astounded me was that Jeremy opened up to me about his whole story from the outset. I stopped him and said, "You know, I could be anybody, paparazzi trying to get a headline."

But he looked at me and said, "You're not; as I have said there's something special about you."

Did Jeremy know back then that there was more to the Imperfectly Perfect Campaign?

For some reason, was he put on my path at that right moment?

IMPERFECTLY PERFECT CAMPAIGN

I did not know then, but it seems so because it has been over six years of brotherhood and nothing but love, support, and help from Jeremy.

That first trip to America introduced me to so many incredible people. I will tell you, the majority of those who helped, and I connected with were from the gym.

Who, like I said, I had got to know them for them.

I never knew many of their professions because, quite frankly, it never came up in conversation.

However, once word got around that gym about what I was trying to do, the community got behind me to spread the efforts, and I will be forever grateful for that.

Building those friendships over the years and finally getting to know their professions, I found out that I had been placed in a community of some of the world's most prominent figures known for their careers. But I was not even aware, nor did I care when I found out who and what so many of them did because I had got to know them for them.

Yes, some could say that surely I recognised a few if they were in Entertainment. But the reality was, nobody was in that industry who I got to know.

And the help from them all paved the way for more trips back to the USA with my efforts.

ONE MAN'S MISSION TO REDEFINE IMPERFECTION
ILLUMINATING THE PATH FORWARD

Returning to Australia after my time in Los Angeles felt like a rude awakening. I had fallen in love with LA—the lifestyle, the people, the culture—and it all resonated with me deeply. I admired and envied the hustle mentality of chasing dreams relentlessly.

So, returning to the grind of a construction site, working long hours six or seven days a week, was a stark contrast to the energy of LA I had been around.

I had taken my photography to LA a couple of years prior, and that hustle mentality and drive I had and still have with the Imperfectly Perfect Campaign, I always credited to the energy and spirit of those I encountered in the USA. They grabbed life by the horns and fearlessly chased their dreams.

Being back home as I toiled away day after day, sacrificing time with my family and trying to continue doing everything I was doing for the efforts, I could not help but wonder when my breakthrough would come. Though I will say despite the frustration and exhaustion at times, I still had an intuitive feeling for what I was doing that persisted. A feeling that what I was doing was meant for

IMPERFECTLY PERFECT CAMPAIGN

even bigger things. I could not quite put my finger on it because it wasn't an easy ride, but I knew deep down that my efforts had to keep going.

One day, a message from Jeremy changed everything.

He shared a picture of himself alongside Eden Sassoon (The Iconic Vidal Sassoon's daughter & Beauty & Wellness Serial Entrepreneur), Justin Guarini (American Idol), and two ladies I was not aware of at the time: Eden Sustin and Kim Somers Egelesee.

He told me that Eden, Justin, and himself had been on the ladies' show and that he had started sharing about the Imperfectly Perfect Campaign when something remarkable transpired.

As Jeremy recounted the experience, he shared that Eden Sassoon had stopped the conversation to share her connection to the phrase "imperfectly perfect," in which she had "perfectly imperfect" tattooed on her arm. Only to say that when getting it done, she was unsure whether she was supposed to put that or, in fact, "imperfectly perfect." Justin Guarini also revealed his affinity for the saying, using it frequently with his children.

Jeremy said the energy in the room had been palpable.

Both Eden and Justin immediately offered their support, becoming integral pillars of the campaign, which they have been for many years now.

There was more to the story, though.

ONE MAN'S MISSION TO REDEFINE IMPERFECTION

Eden and Kim, who hosted the podcast, were both highly spiritual. Eden being an evidential medium, and Kim, an intuitive.

A few days after Jeremy's message, I felt compelled to reach out to them. To my surprise, our connection was instantaneous, and they revealed something extraordinary during our conversation.

See, they confirmed what Jeremy had mentioned about the energy in the room being palpable and how it had shifted dramatically, with bright purple light filling the space when the Imperfectly Perfect Campaign was mentioned.

They explained that they were being shown that my work with the Imperfectly Perfect Campaign was divinely guided. They asked if I would be open to a channelled session with them both. I agreed because, well, I was more than intrigued. I was open to anything.

We set up a call the following week, and I listened as revelations came through in the session. One was about the significance of the colour purple that had filled the room. They revealed that the late artist Prince had come forward to guide this journey and that the colour purple was how he presented himself. But not only did Prince come through, but also Chester Bennington.

I found myself at a loss for words. It was a lot to take in—too much, in fact.

IMPERFECTLY PERFECT CAMPAIGN

How was I supposed to believe that two of the world's most prolific artists were actively coming forth in a session to me, who nobody knew, guiding me and this mission?

Even despite being told things that Eden and Kim could never have known, I could not shake the scepticism that crept in. This was all so new, so surreal. I struggled to reconcile the enormity of what was unfolding with the reality of my doubts.

Eden assured me that those who had presented themselves would provide evidence to support their claims. But even so, I could not help but feel sceptical.

How could I, here I was, Glenn, with no prior experience in any of what I was doing nor having any idea about anything spiritual at all, be expected to 'believe' that I had been given such a monumental task that was apparently being "guided" and pushed by Prince and Chester Bennington?

ONE MAN'S MISSION TO REDEFINE IMPERFECTION
NAVIGATING COLLABORATION AND COMPETITION

The revelations that my efforts were being spiritually guided naturally piqued my curiosity. I found myself seeking more, although I needed to figure out where or how to find it. Weeks and months passed, and everything surrounding my mission was running smoothly.

Since America, I can keep repeating that even more public figures were getting involved and sharing their support; more coverage from publications and networks kept coming, and the efforts were across all social media, with everybody sharing it.

Furthermore, behind the scenes, I was moving, weaving, connecting, keeping everything updated, sending out press releases, and pushing forward.

Now, something new that people around me suggested, was to start contacting others in the space and explore collaborations. Simple ways to join forces and make one enormous impact together.

IMPERFECTLY PERFECT CAMPAIGN

This experience served yet another lesson waiting to be learned. Let me be candid here: while building the Imperfectly Perfect Campaign, I was admittedly naive in many aspects. However, one area where my naivety persisted for far too long was in the way of people.

What I eventually discovered was that even within the realm of others aiming to "advocate," there exists a significant degree of competition—a reality I had failed to acknowledge.

Why would I?

I had often heard the sentiment that individuals on missions to aid others should unite. Yet, the reality I encountered was far different on two occasions.

It became evident that while some may express willingness to collaborate, their underlying motivations may be driven by competition. In retrospect, I should have anticipated such experiences.

Nevertheless, I remained unaware, failing to recognise the competitive dynamics.

This was my first experience in reaching out to others that were making similar efforts. The first "red flag" I did not see was that those who said "sure, let's do it" never truly put any effort in.

I found myself organising meetings, discussing what we could do together, and found myself moving things along. Otherwise, in

ONE MAN'S MISSION TO REDEFINE IMPERFECTION

all honesty, I do not think anything would have come from the collaboration.

The second "red flag" I never saw or had even thought of was not putting something in writing to ensure that all parties were equally promoting everything we were doing in terms of what and how we were collaborating to make a difference.

So, this was me at the time.

Naive and only thinking of how we could do something for the betterment of others.

I had suggested bringing one of their representatives on to the Imperfectly Perfect Campaign's efforts to capture a portrait with a collaborative message that we could all promote and get out to people. They were more than happy with this.

In the first week of my posting everything all over the Imperfectly Perfect Campaign's platforms (remember, this is the time while all of the press attention was on the Imperfectly Perfect Campaign's efforts and many were watching, across all of our platforms, including journalists and producers) and tagging, plus directing people to the other organisation's mission and efforts, not one single post came from them.

I sent a couple of messages to follow up, but I was met with silence. I did not see or hear anything about the Imperfectly Perfect Campaign.

IMPERFECTLY PERFECT CAMPAIGN

However, ironically, several weeks later, I saw an active post pop up across the other's socials with the exact same message we had drawn up as a collective, posted as their own with no mention of the Imperfectly Perfect Campaign.

Was this another instance of people leveraging my achievements to promote their agendas? It certainly seemed that way. Oh, but I am not finished there.

It was like this one month; I was learning harsh realities fast.

A publication was also about to run a full spread on the Imperfectly Perfect Campaign's efforts around this time.

However, before the launch date, I received a call from a friend who shared some news with me. The publication was no longer running the article on the Imperfectly Perfect Campaign. Still, it was going to run an article with another organisation in the same field. I asked my friend if this was what normally happens, especially after getting confirmation from the publication.

They had said not typically if everything had already been confirmed, gone through the editor, and was ready to be released.

However, my friend then asked me if I had spoken to anybody about the article before it was released. I mentioned only one person I had in the week leading up to it. I knew the person in question was an advocate for another organisation, but why would that matter? They were also doing amazing things in the space, and

ONE MAN'S MISSION TO REDEFINE IMPERFECTION

I did not think anything of telling them the exciting news about this particular publication running the story.

My friend asked me who the person was.

Upon telling them, I was only then told that the person I had mentioned my news to was not just an advocate for the organisation, but somebody exceptionally well known, who worked alongside the other organisation, and would have direct contacts with that very publication.

Again, I may never know. It looks ironic that I spoke with this person only a few days before. The next minute, the publication drops the article on the Imperfectly Perfect Campaign and goes with the very organisation that the 'other person' was attached to.

Four times now!

Yet it still seemed I needed to fully grasp the lesson when dealing with people.

But do you know what?

Looking back, I cannot and will not judge myself harshly.

I know once more that I needed these situations to unfold.

Initially, to see if I had learned from the first and second times—clearly, I had not. Secondly, to start gaining more discernment on people who may 'appear' to have your best interests at heart and realise they may not have.

IMPERFECTLY PERFECT CAMPAIGN

Both experiences taught me to be cautious about sharing my plans with anybody and to always double down on doing my due diligence on others. Lastly, I needed to start ensuring that everything was documented in writing if I were to collaborate with anybody in the future.

ONE MAN'S MISSION TO REDEFINE IMPERFECTION
TOUCHED BY THE DIVINE

After reading my words, you must have thought by now, "Wow, not only was Glenn naive and trusting, but some may say very gullible."

But I would also hope you have thought along the way: "Wow, that is somebody with the determination to keep walking through the storms no matter what has been thrown at him."

As I write these words, know what I have shared thus far is only a glimpse of my experiences that you have read about. Yet even the ones I have mentioned, I can, in hindsight, see that getting through all these experiences was about having faith all along.

Would these 'experiences' that kept showing up make me keep going or lose 'faith' in what had been placed on my heart?

Now, I have shared some of the not-so-nice experiences, which all served as lessons, and equally shared that through them, the wrong people were brought along my path.

But I must be equally grateful for some of the most amazing people who have come along my path at this time, too. When you

IMPERFECTLY PERFECT CAMPAIGN

have something big placed on your heart, you will need those fantastic people around you.

Those who see you for you, those who want to know you, and those who genuinely have your back, who also have experience in what you are going through and can pick you up when it feels like you are falling.

Michael Falzon.

I remember the first time I met Michael for the campaign. He immediately supported my efforts and invited me to the Sydney Opera House, where he was starring in the musical Evita alongside Tina Arena.

We hit it off from the get-go.

There was just a purity about him.

To know that I was in the presence of one of Australia's most prolific musical 'legends', his humbleness and sincerity just shone so brightly. He wanted to know more about the campaign and me. It was honestly refreshing. I remember the day like it was yesterday.

We shot Michael's portrait for the campaign outside the iconic Opera House. Still, Michael asked if I had ever been inside the building, to which I responded that I had not. So, he invited me behind the scenes of the show. He introduced me to several cast members and even took me to the main stage to see how

ONE MAN'S MISSION TO REDEFINE IMPERFECTION

spectacular the Opera House was inside. It was amazing; honestly, he did not have to do that. But that is who I came to find out Michael was.

Over the months, we shot several short projects for the campaign, including an incredible and funny podcast episode alongside another of Australia's prominent TV personalities and journalists, Michelle Stephenson, where I learned even more about Michael.

The conversations always delved deep, and there was just something about him: his energy built those around him.

Not just through projects, but Michael, again, who did not have to, reached out to me often and checked in on me. He frequently asked me how I was doing. He ensured that while I was taking on this mission and everybody's energy, I was also being supported. He often said he was only a call away if I needed to speak to somebody. It is something I will always be grateful to Michael for.

He taught me the importance of making sure that people were pouring into me equally with support as much as I was pouring out to everybody else.

In July of the same year, Michael simply messaged one morning and said, "Do you mind if I head to the studio to share some news on the campaign?"

IMPERFECTLY PERFECT CAMPAIGN

Of course, it was ok, but for what he was about to share, nobody was prepared to hear. He told everybody that he had been diagnosed with a rare form of cancer but that he was in great spirits, that they had caught it early, and that he wanted to reassure everybody he was fighting this thing. It honestly took my breath away.

At a time when he should have been thinking about himself, he thought of others by sharing his diagnosis and sending thoughts and reassurance to those who all knew him.

I also could not go far without mentioning Eden and Kim, who became spiritual mentors to me, Jeremy, my brother, and Rachael Newsham, too. They all became extended family members, quite literally. They became 'those' people to me.

I spoke earlier about the 'connection' with Jeremy and how he, Eden, and Kim were brought onto my path, but Rachael, let me just say right here.

I can only look back and say, like Jeremy, Eden, and Kim, that our meeting was not by coincidence but was clearly divinely guided and meant to be.

Let me share something with you.

Here is somebody through a group fitness program by Les Mills International that I followed for a number of years through the

ONE MAN'S MISSION TO REDEFINE IMPERFECTION

screens. Alongside her partner in crime, Dan Cohen, as Program Director for the international exercise program, Body Combat.

I admired, looked up to, and aspired to be like both, just as many millions around the world did and still do to this day. I was based in the UK then, following them both being based in New Zealand (albeit both pommes).

Let me briefly remind you of something here.

Remember when I got offered the job in the gym after using my voice to stand up for my colleagues in the hospitality establishment and got let go?

Through all that, I started my fitness career in that gym, first at the front desk and moving on to the gym floor. Then, I fell in love with Group Fitness, which started me on a journey to teach Dan and Rachael's program, Body Combat.

I have to say here that this book would go on for a long time if I continued to share all the tangents of my story that are attributed to things like this, but I am trying to keep an exceptionally long story short!

In a nutshell, my parents had divorced years earlier, my mum had gone on to find a new partner several years later, and they decided to move to New Zealand. At the time, I was teaching a lot in the UK, had just moved out of home, and was enjoying my early twenties with friends.

IMPERFECTLY PERFECT CAMPAIGN

But my mum then threw a spanner in the works. Would I like to join them and try a new country, heading to New Zealand, or would I prefer to stay in the UK?

In truth, it was a hard decision. I loved my job in fitness, going out with my close group of friends, and having it easy at the time.

But then here comes the opportunity to head to New Zealand, of all places!

Who is in New Zealand? Les Mills. What program is? Body Combat and who are the program directors? Dan and Rachael?

You will have heard people, no doubt, who have often spoken of always knowing that they were meant for other places. That, albeit loving where they were from, due to friends and familiarity, they always knew they would end up somewhere else.

That was me.

Although, like I say, I loved where I was from, I just simply always knew I would not be there forever. I knew I would not marry a local girl. I knew I would not start a family there, and I knew something out there in the world was waiting for me. More than anything that where I was from could offer me.

However, I should have researched my geography to see where Rachael and Dan were in New Zealand. Blonde moment!

I ended up in Christchurch, and they were based in Auckland!

ONE MAN'S MISSION TO REDEFINE IMPERFECTION

Now, I said this was trying to cut a long story short but bear with me; I am trying to get to the bulk of this story fast.

My mum and her partner moved back to the UK a year and a half later because my sister had a baby, and my mum wanted to be close by. I decided to stay on.

I loved New Zealand, travelled, lived with, and met people from all over the world daily. I not only became an avid member of Les Mills International in Christchurch but also had the opportunity to teach amongst and learn from the best of the best while there.

Once my visa for New Zealand ran out, I had two choices: move back to the UK or head towards Australia.

I chose Australia, where everything seemed to fall in my favour. I fell straight into a group of friends, a new apartment, and a job in the fitness industry, which led me straight into teaching there.

I began teaching all around Sydney and loving every moment of it. I worked during the day in sales for the gym, worked around my shifts teaching classes, and headed to the beach with friends. This was the life.

As I told you, I was still in my twenties here, and there was no sign that Body Dysmorphia was around the corner for me.

Funnily enough, it was also when I picked up a camera and started shooting anything and everything. You see from an early

IMPERFECTLY PERFECT CAMPAIGN

age; I remember loving photography and even ended my school's final exams shooting a whole presentation through visual mediums.

But like with most things when you are growing up, hobbies change, and you seem to need to remember what you used to be passionate about.

Travelling and being into fitness seemed to get me fired back up to start shooting once more, and so I did. Serendipitously, one event for Les Mills Asia Pacific came to Sydney, and something told me to take my camera.

I started shooting in and around the event and, unexpectedly, was approached by a Les Mills representative who asked if they could see the images after the event. Fast-forward. I then became an official photographer at their Sydney-based events. Lo and behold, both Rachael and Dan got to know me from afar behind the lens at the time.

About a year later, as the Imperfectly Perfect Campaign continued to gain momentum, I felt compelled to contact Rachael and share what I was trying to accomplish with my efforts. To my delight, she immediately embraced the cause and rallied the support of the other Les Mills Programme Directors too.

From that moment on, Rachael remained steadfast by my side, not just as a supporter but as a friend and an integral part of my extended family, just like Jeremy, Michael, Eden, and Kim.

ONE MAN'S MISSION TO REDEFINE IMPERFECTION

Regardless of the challenges I have faced and will recount in my story moving forward, I have always found solace in the unwavering support of these fantastic people.

They have been my pillars of strength, always ready to catch me when I felt like I had fallen. They poured encouragement into me and shared so much wisdom, having had similar experiences along their journey that always meant the world to me, as did each of them and still do.

IMPERFECTLY PERFECT CAMPAIGN
THE END OF A NAIVE HEART

As we approached the year-and-a-half mark, the external facade of the Imperfectly Perfect Campaign seemed to shimmer with consistency, and the campaign's reach surged with momentum. Yet, behind the scenes, I was still labouring in construction and pouring myself into every aspect to keep things moving forward. Though the irony was palpable.

Requests often flooded in, asking me through the Imperfectly Perfect Campaign to sponsor events or support various causes.

Friends even reached out numerous times, seeking endorsements to share their efforts in raising money for other charities or asking me to connect them with celebrities for things like wishing people happy birthdays.

It was almost comical that everybody bypassed the fact that I was leading by being so transparent across social media about everything I was doing.

A defining moment came towards 'people' when an experience opened my eyes to the stark reality of giving too much and the vast difference between words and actions.

ONE MAN'S MISSION TO REDEFINE IMPERFECTION

Somebody I had connected with, a great person by all accounts, eagerly jumped on board with my efforts. However, after a few weeks, they approached me, expressing a desire to connect with a celebrity who they had seen was into the same sport as them, lived close to them, and had said to me that it would be great if I could connect them so that they could possibly go and do a session together.

Oblivious to any ulterior motives, I simply facilitated the connection. Only to discover weeks later that the celebrity was suddenly endorsing the person's product – a fact conveniently omitted from the initial conversation by the person wanting to be introduced to the celebrity.

Now, it was amazing to see the celebrity gaining opportunities like this, do not get me wrong. They had no idea what had transpired behind the scenes. How I was approached by a seemingly innocent connection from somebody wanting to do a session in the sport they shared a passion for.

At that moment, it once again hit me like a ton of bricks. Was I just being used again, this time as a free resource for connections to promote somebody's products?

Do you realise how much money is involved in product endorsements and how often companies don't have direct connections to celebrities?

IMPERFECTLY PERFECT CAMPAIGN

Yet here I was, Glenn, now seemingly, being seen as a free resource for introductions to celebrities!

Wow!

It was a wake-up call, that was for sure, and one that prompted me to confront the naivety that had coloured many of my interactions thus far. It was the time I finally said enough is enough.

I confronted the individual, questioning their true intentions and asking why they had not been honest with me. I also asked where my product was – a tangible reminder of the value I brought to the table.

Let's just say, I did not receive anything.

From that point on, I resolved to shed my naivety and sharpen my business acumen, especially when dealing with people. I delved into psychology literature, studied the intricacies of human behaviour in business settings, and devoured podcasts on discernment and shrewdness in dealings.

I also reflected on my patterns of behaviour when opening doors for others, probing whether they stemmed from a misguided sense of gratitude. After all, if I had this misguided sense of gratitude that I had to do things for others because they supported my efforts, I would be thinking about it all the wrong way.

Where had this notion even come from?

ONE MAN'S MISSION TO REDEFINE IMPERFECTION

This was the fifth time I had found myself in a comparable situation, and it was clear that I needed to change my approach quickly.

It was time to work smarter and be vigilant in discerning genuine connections from opportunistic ones. I knew that this turning point would shape my interactions and decisions moving forward, and it was.

The new Glenn stepped forward!

IMPERFECTLY PERFECT CAMPAIGN
WHEN DOUBT CREEPS IN

Though I was stepping forward as a new man.

Before we move forward, I want to share about how many of these previous experiences affected me at the time. Like I said, I have shared numerous experiences already, and trust me, there are plenty more to come, albeit dealt with very differently. But to authentically convey my truths through this book, which I hope will inspire others to resonate, I feel it necessary to delve into how much I struggled with self-judgment, self-criticism, and pulling myself down upon going through many of the experiences.

We can all wear this bravado, this mask of, 'I'm tough, I can handle it.' But honestly, experiences like that are pretty rubbish.

As I reflect on the experiences and their takeaways throughout each chapter, as I have mentioned, I realise that they were meant to happen as blessings for my growth. However, without detailing the actual feelings of going through those experiences at those particular times, I'd do the book and its readers, you, an injustice.

ONE MAN'S MISSION TO REDEFINE IMPERFECTION

As you read about my naivety and gullibility, it is essential to understand the inner turmoil I faced. I will be honest—sometimes, I felt like a complete idiot. There's a fine line between leading with a good heart and being taken advantage of due to one's naivety.

If you have ever experienced something similar, you'll understand the constant questioning:

Am I that stupid?

Can I even do this?

Am I that thick?

It is a battle against cynicism while grappling with self-doubt. I was my harshest critic. Despite sacrificing so much time away from family and friends to help others, doubts would plague my mind.

Why am I doing this?

Am I just a fool giving without receiving?

Do people also see me as an idiot?

Do people just think, 'Oh, it's Glenn, he'll be fine if we use him'?

These questions loomed large, especially when I saw many taking from me while I freely gave.

Even after all this time of navigating this journey, the emotional and mental toll of self-doubt would creep in during those very experiences. Because I thought, maybe I was just stupid for continuing to:

IMPERFECTLY PERFECT CAMPAIGN

A: Not see them.

B: Repeat the same patterns.

The internal struggles were compounded by the physical demands of working long hours in construction to support my family and keep everything going. This last experience of being used as a mere free resource for connections shattered the pattern that had plagued me for so long.

It was a pivotal moment, forcing me to confront the outdated narrative of self-doubt and self-criticism that had pervaded my thoughts. I realised that instead of asking why the universe or God was subjecting me to these trials, and doing it to me, I should ask what lessons I could glean from them and why they were happening for me.

With a change in how I perceived these experiences and seeing them as happening for my good, answers started becoming obvious to me. Each experience, however unpleasant, served as a stepping stone forward. They tested my resilience, faith, and determination to keep moving despite obstacles. They were not punishments inflicted upon me but rather opportunities. With each setback, I grew more robust, resilient, and determined to fulfil the mission in my heart.

ONE MAN'S MISSION TO REDEFINE IMPERFECTION

These experiences shaped me into the person I needed to be to navigate the challenges ahead and realise the full potential of the mission entrusted to me.

IMPERFECTLY PERFECT CAMPAIGN
FORTIFYING THE HEART

It became apparent that the last experience had indeed opened my eyes and begun to shape me into a new person. So, unbeknownst to them, I thank the person who did that for me this day. Even though the doors were well and truly closed for them after that, I held no animosity. I wished them well and knew that I was grateful for what they had taught me.

I was no longer willing to fall prey to the patterns of being used or overlooked or succumb to my naivety. With newfound confidence, I began setting clear boundaries and asserting myself in ways I never knew I could.

For the ongoing months, I set people straight immediately, put firm boundaries in place, and developed confidence in myself more than I knew I had in me.

I am sure you are waiting to hear one of those stories… right?

Here you go.

One experience occurred through LinkedIn with an acquaintance I had gotten to know through my networking events. I am sure they saw an energy of naivety around me at some point, too, which is why they tried what they did with me but failed miserably.

The individual in question suggested that we do a mutual event where we would speak about our services and share the programs that we offered. It confused me slightly, as I knew that this person was fully aware that I was not a coach and was never trying to push a program.

So, did they mean we would be rolling out a joint program of some sort together?

The person said, "Oh, you should promote what you are doing, and I will promote what I'm doing."

Something was amiss, but I decided to let them speak.

They tried to control the narrative, saying how it should go, detailing that since I was great at bringing people together, I should organise the event, and that they could then facilitate.

I saw where this was going.

I questioned whether there would be a referral fee if I brought everyone to the event and they sold their program and if people should sign up for it.

After all, if I was to be putting an audience in front of them for free and doing all the work in marketing the event to attract those people, then surely.

IMPERFECTLY PERFECT CAMPAIGN

I remember them saying, "Glenn, you have to remember there are enough clients in the world to go around, and I don't give referral fees."

I simply responded, "Funny that because I thought you were an abundance coach. And knowing this, wouldn't you agree that there is enough money to go around, too?"

There was little to say, and silence ensued. Only one message later that same week wishing me well in my endeavours.

I never heard from the person again, nor did I see them show up to any of my networking events, which was ironic because they had never missed one before this.

Alas, like I said, those several months were when I took time to really hone in and study Human Psychology and Behavioural Patterns, as well as start leaning more into those intuitive 'feelings' that had kept creeping up, as I've mentioned in my story.

In all honesty, it truly helped me.

I became privy to a lot to assert myself. Through asserting myself and finally stepping up, it was like I broke a pattern that I was so accustomed to, that I realised there was nobody to blame but myself. I was keeping myself in it.

So, for those of you who feel a sense of resonating with my words right now, I will say right here: patterns like these will keep showing up for you until you do something about them

ONE MAN'S MISSION TO REDEFINE IMPERFECTION
FINDING CLARITY IN THE UNEXPECTED

Detailing day-by-day accounts of my journey is challenging because, well, frankly, there has been so much to navigate. So, I must recollect the times by using stories from particular years.

Do you know how hard that is? Especially when you are getting older.

That aside, I hope anybody reading thus far is learning that having something placed on your heart to make a difference in this world does not come easily.

Social media and 'highlights' often make things look easy, but it is simply not the reality.

People only see the 'tip of the iceberg' with what I have managed to achieve, even when I share the transparency of what it has taken. But people will still choose to see the public figures on board, the publicity and coverage, all that stuff. Still, they will never truly see below the surface for many reasons.

IMPERFECTLY PERFECT CAMPAIGN

Maybe they just don't want to see it. Perhaps they think it can't be that hard, or maybe they think it's just luck. I am not here to claim I know any other person's thoughts about how they perceive or look at something, though. All I can say is that society has done an excellent job of making so many see the way they 'think' something is or even how 'somebody' is.

ONE MAN'S MISSION TO REDEFINE IMPERFECTION
WHEN THE SIGNS ALIGN

Enter 2020 – a year that no one anticipated. It brought with it a global pandemic that disrupted lives and livelihoods on an unprecedented scale. The onset of the pandemic posed significant challenges for everyone, forcing a pause on many fronts.

For an initiative centred around human connection and photography, adapting to this new reality meant rethinking how to maintain community engagement and support. This period prompted a profound shift in my approach.

I started turning even more to digital platforms, leveraging podcasts, social media, and virtual events to foster that connection and provide free resources for people. From virtual events to interactive live sessions, I sought to keep the spirit of the Imperfectly Perfect Campaign alive despite the physical distance imposed by the pandemic.

And yes, I was still pouring my money into keeping everything running. It was suggested that I start getting some support apparel out there to ease the pressure of spending money on everything.

IMPERFECTLY PERFECT CAMPAIGN

Like many, I stumbled upon an unexpected haven of solace and inspiration amidst the chaos and uncertainty of the pandemic: Clubhouse, an audio-based social networking app.

Initially dismissing it as just another digital platform, I soon discovered its profound potential as a catalyst for networking, spiritual exploration, and revelation, which I was truly beginning to seek more of, especially after what had been happening.

One evening, I found myself drawn to a virtual gathering led by a renowned shaman. Participants were encouraged to focus on a card drawn from a pack and share their intuitive insights. Despite my initial scepticism, I approached the exercise with an open mind, driven by a desire to uncover hidden truths and deepen my own understanding of spirituality.

But I could not see anything. I could not intuitively feel anything, so something within me prompted me to 'virtually raise my hand' on the platform. The app is virtual, and people can only see 'profiles' in networking rooms. There is the ability to see people's profiles on screen, as the 'speakers' on stage and audience members present in the room.

You may be brought up onto the 'virtual stage' if you raise your hand. That I was. I was invited onto the 'virtual' stage and asked to look at the card 'before' me.

Clearly, I was in my head from the onset.

ONE MAN'S MISSION TO REDEFINE IMPERFECTION

The shaman caught me off guard, urging me to relax and refrain from delving too deeply into my logical mind. Yet despite my best efforts, I found myself grappling with uncertainty, even thinking if I should merely feign seeing something to avoid making others feel awkward.

It was a perplexing moment, then heightened by the shaman's request to 'tap' into my energy by placing a 'burning sensation' somewhere on my body, to which I had to let him know when I felt it and where.

I agreed, albeit unsure of what to expect.

I mean, come on. Here I was, sitting in my room in Australia, legs crossed, phone in hand, on a virtual event with people and a shaman from other areas of the world.

What was I to think? I awaited the unfolding of this mysterious encounter.

Suddenly, a faint sensation of heat pricked my right shoulder blade, signalling the shaman's intervention. I let him know. He asked if he could intensify the heat. I agreed.

My arms suddenly began to move involuntarily, a strange movement by forces beyond my comprehension. The virtual room had a comments section that showed on the screen. It erupted with astonishment as those in the room shared their marvel at what was happening.

IMPERFECTLY PERFECT CAMPAIGN

Amidst the chaos, the shaman probed further, amplifying the sensations until my fingers suddenly started to dance with an unseen rhythm. It was like they had a mind of their own and were typing something in front of my very own eyes.

Bewildered, I still struggled to comprehend the significance of what was happening.

It was then that the shaman bestowed upon me a title I could not fathom – he said that what everybody was bearing witness to was being in the presence of a Celestial Code Writer.

I listened but, at the same time, found myself blurting out,

'What the bloody hell is a Celestial Code Writer?'

I listened to the shaman's description of a 'Celestial Code Writer,' being somebody who had the ability to change the matrix.

Know what I said one more time? You may have guessed it,

'What the bloody hell is the Matrix?'

What did all of it mean?

As the moment sank in, I received an outpouring of messages from those in the room once more, affirming the authenticity of the experience.

I received messages from those who also channelled, other mediums, and intuitive, all pouring into me and telling me that I needed to understand the enormity of what was before me. Their words echoed the shaman's proclamation, urging me to delve

ONE MAN'S MISSION TO REDEFINE IMPERFECTION

deeper into my spiritual side. Yet it was a revelation that shook the foundations of my understanding, propelling me further along the enigmatic path ahead.

As more people seemingly stepped forward, leading me to grasp that there's more to this world and what I was doing was being guided, it still became a hard pill to swallow.

Even with wanting to explore and seeing many serendipitous experiences happening around me, I would be lying if I said it was easy to shake off what society had ingrained in me, as it has everybody – questioning if this was real or just a load of baloney.

During much of the pandemic, the Clubhouse app became a place to seek. Entering networking rooms allowed me to listen to other people's spiritual journeys, walks in faith, and experiences in their personal and professional lives. In moments like these, I also decided to seek more knowledge in the professional realm on the app towards facets of business that I knew I needed to start leaning into.

Through the app, I met some incredible individuals with whom I am still close to this day, but it also became apparent that in so many of the 'business rooms,' it was more about who spun tales of earning exorbitant amounts of money, who offered discounted programs, and who showcased lifestyles that seemed too good to be true to everybody.

IMPERFECTLY PERFECT CAMPAIGN

Many of the so-called business rooms I entered became increasingly about smoke and mirrors.

I decided to utilise the platform for my spiritual journey.

I laugh because it was not long before I witnessed a whole smoke and mirror façade in so many of these spiritual and faith-based rooms, too.

While I tried to remain open-minded in many of the rooms I entered, I could not ignore the red flags that kept creeping up.

For instance, in several rooms I was entering surrounding faith, the hosts, aka the 'man or woman' of God, claimed to be hearing the word of God. But suddenly, started insisting that everybody in the room needed to pour money into their PayPal or Venmo accounts to receive their blessings.

It baffled me how people, devoid of faith and divine connection, could believe and continue to pour into these hosts' demands, thinking God would be telling this one person the exact amount of money that every single person had to give to them.

I mean, God was apparently saying it had to be poured directly into the source of the room. Not to give somebody who may need that money who indeed may be deserving and struggling?

More supposed spaces of spiritual enlightenment, I began encountering similar individuals who sought to exploit others for personal gain. It was just mind-blowing to me.

ONE MAN'S MISSION TO REDEFINE IMPERFECTION

What was more disheartening was witnessing or hearing people on the app, desperate for guidance and blessings, fall prey to it all. I witnessed a lot, and I even had men and women of faith slide into my messages via social media, claiming to have messages from a higher power. Only to reveal their true intentions – expecting me to pour money into them.

Moreover, in other instances, I observed more individuals of faith who, despite their own shortcomings, took it upon themselves to chastise others for living lifestyles deemed "unrighteous."

The irony was glaring – they preached salvation while condemning others without empathy or understanding. Instead of sharing their stories of redemption, they chose to judge and condemn, further tarnishing the image of faith and spirituality.

Thankfully, after witnessing so many of these instances, I suddenly began stumbling upon rooms of faith and spiritual practice, where integrity and morals actually seemed to have been held with high regard, and discussions about these false narratives and manipulative tactics were openly addressed of which I had been witnessing.

Rooms that genuinely made a profound impact on me, as did the men and women I got to know and give praise to.

Again, reflecting on that time, it was as if I was being shown what to be careful of, what to look out for, and how to start gaining

IMPERFECTLY PERFECT CAMPAIGN

discernment in knowing that not everybody who claims to be of faith or spirituality in this world truly is.

Once I was shown this, it was as if doors were opened to direct me to those who showed me what a genuinely spiritual, faith-based path was meant to be about.

And that reaffirmed my commitment to seeking truth, integrity, and genuine connection throughout everything.

ONE MAN'S MISSION TO REDEFINE IMPERFECTION
THE UNENDING SEARCH FOR TRUTH

As the pandemic gripped the world, instilling fear in the hearts and minds of people everywhere, its impact on employment was profound. Being entrenched in the construction industry, I felt the reverberations firsthand as work sites ground to a halt and tools were laid down. With responsibilities weighing heavily on my shoulders—a mortgage to pay and family to support—the logical next step was to explore online job opportunities.

Remember, the Imperfectly Perfect Campaign did not have people pouring into it to make it sustainable, let alone cover anything other than some amazing people purchasing apparel, which did not cover much. It was still predominantly all on me.

So, turning to platforms like Seek in Australia, I sought remote positions that could be done from home. Thankfully, my sporadic construction work had provided some financial stability, supplemented by my wife's ability to work remotely. Despite not being in immediate financial distress, I continued to cast my net wide, applying for various roles.

IMPERFECTLY PERFECT CAMPAIGN

To my surprise, I received a call one morning about a marketing position at an organisation I could not recall applying to. Marketing was not my forte, nor something that would have stood out on my resume, and working for a non-profit organisation certainly wasn't something I had considered, so I was baffled by how this came to me.

However, the conversation went well, and the role seemed promising. After three days of silence, I reached out for an update, only to learn that the position had been filled. Nevertheless, to my surprise, they suddenly offered a more senior role leading their business development team — an unexpected turn of events that I accepted.

Despite my initial reservations, I threw myself into the role, embracing the opportunity to work from home. However, when starting the position, I always felt an intuitive feeling gnawing at me, consistently hinting that my tenure would be short-lived. True to that intuition, six months later, I found myself correct.

While the experience was invaluable and the team supportive, I could not shake the feeling that something didn't align. The inner workings of seeing how non-profit organisations worked revealed a disconnect between my values and the prevailing politics I was learning about.

ONE MAN'S MISSION TO REDEFINE IMPERFECTION

Reflecting on this experience and seeking guidance from a trusted friend known for her intuitive insights, I could not help but tell her my ever-prevailing thoughts while I was there.

I felt I had been 'placed' in the role to learn an essential lesson for this journey of mine toward serving a higher purpose. I cannot help but repeat my feelings through my story as 'blowing my mind' as confirmation from my friend loomed large, validating my innermost convictions.

I was told that the feelings of uneasiness around commencing a non-profit throughout my journey thus far were being shown to me each step of the way through the experiences I had been put through. Being 'placed' within a non-profit organisation was the final confirmation as to why I was not to start one.

The Imperfectly Perfect Campaign was different. It was being divinely led away from conventional paths and towards a destiny defined by authenticity, 'not of this world,' as she had said.

During my tenure with the organisation, I could not ignore the ominous undercurrents shaping the world around us. Even from the confines of home offices, it was evident that employment rights were being eroded with the pressure to receive this sudden vaccine for COVID-19.

Fear permeated every facet of society, with those who chose not to vaccinate facing exclusion and ostracization. Let me clarify—I

IMPERFECTLY PERFECT CAMPAIGN

was never an anti-vaxxer, as the prevailing narrative would have it. However, what unfolded before my eyes was a stark illustration of societal division and coercion on an unprecedented scale.

Families were torn apart, friendships strained, all over personal choices and rights. It was a distressing time, marked by a pervasive "us vs. them" mentality.

Despite my reservations, I grappled with the decision as pressure mounted. Even close friends succumbed to the societal pressure, their choices influenced by government mandates and restrictions on daily life.

Yet, that intuitive nudge grew stronger within me, whispering that something was amiss here, too. As the vaccination drive intensified, so too did my unease. The disparity between the public narrative and the realities on the ground became increasingly apparent.

Politicians who championed strict protocols for the masses were exposed for flouting regulations at clandestine parties. Government mandates, telling people to socially distance themselves and wear masks; otherwise, they would be fined, were sparking controversy by being caught around people who did not adhere to social distancing and did not wear masks themselves - a stark betrayal of public trust.

ONE MAN'S MISSION TO REDEFINE IMPERFECTION

Now, I acknowledge that COVID-19 was, by all means, a real threat and have never dismissed its importance. However, how this 'sudden' vaccination was enforced and pervasive propaganda put out left a bitter taste in my mouth.

I witnessed firsthand the toll it took on mental health, exacerbated by the relentless push for compliance. What also troubled me was seeing the commodification of mental health advocacy, exemplified by an organisation's apparel partnership promoting the slogan "get vaxxed."

At a time when mental health was plummeting, and adverse reactions to the vaccine were also emerging, this felt truly odd for an organisation focusing on such an important topic to take sides. It made me question whether they were compelled to be complicit due to funding, aligning themselves with the pushed narrative.

Now, as employment rights everywhere were tightening and friends around me were seemingly all getting vaccinated for an 'easier' life, I finally ignored that intuitive nudge and succumbed. I decided there was no choice other than to get vaccinated.

My wife, classified as a frontline worker since the start of the pandemic, received her vaccine early on. Initially, I was offered the vaccination as her partner. Still, as I mentioned, something felt amiss, and that intuitive nudge urged me to decline.

IMPERFECTLY PERFECT CAMPAIGN

Anyway, I had now bypassed that nudge because everything around me seemed insurmountable, and I saw no way around it. So, I drove to the hospital during the week.

I had never really spoken to God in a full-blown fashion before. This day, I spoke to God.

I was asking to be protected and even said if I am not to have this, make the needle drop to the floor, or make no parking available as I get to the hospital. I was panicking, I'll admit it.

But I drove there, found a spot, waited for my vaccine, and the needle did not drop. Damn!

After the jab, I was told to wait 10-15 minutes in the waiting room alongside others. This was apparently to see if anybody had a reaction. It was not a pleasant feeling at all.

Two weeks passed, and during work meetings, I recall a few team members saying they had been experiencing migraines more than ever, and I simply mentioned I had been having bouts of a tight chest. One of my colleagues reached out to check in on me, as they had been hearing several people having similar issues after the jab.

But it was not until that weekend that my family and I were sitting at home watching a movie and having takeout when my chest didn't feel right; I was almost experiencing palpitations. Something was off.

ONE MAN'S MISSION TO REDEFINE IMPERFECTION

I said to my wife that I thought I should go to the hospital. With the kids not ready for bed for long, after the movie and food, I said, "I'll be fine, I'll go." The whole way there, I was nervous.

This was odd. I was fit, I trained, I was healthy, what was happening?

I remember sitting in the reception waiting with others to be seen. Masks were everywhere, and people were told to keep their distance.

I was frantically texting my friends of faith to pray for me. I was honestly scared. I also texted friends and anybody until I realised my battery was running low. The hospital had a charging port in the waiting area, so I walked over.

I noticed that the only spare lead I picked up had a slight casing defect on the wire. As I went to grab it, I had a sudden jolt hit me, an electric shock that made me jump back.

God knows what the others in the waiting area thought.

I went to sit back down, with even more trepidation now, thinking about my heart. What have I done?

The nurse came to get me and asked me what was going on. I went on to explain, and what shocked me the most was what she said.

"We have been seeing quite a lot lately with chest complaints since the vaccination."

IMPERFECTLY PERFECT CAMPAIGN

"Oh great," I thought.

She took me through tests, Echo, ECG, and blood. I was hooked up to leads, I was prodded, everything. Then, there was a long wait until the doctor came to call my name back in the waiting room.

What happened next was strange as I sat waiting for what seemed like hours. The tightness and palpitations I had felt dissipated.

When the doctor finally called my name and reviewed all my results, they were next to perfect. Not one single issue or elevated heart rate, anything. Part of me thought the doctor must have thought I was a bloody hypochondriac.

As I left the hospital, my friend PK called me back. With him being in the USA, it would have been late. But I proceeded to tell him I had been calling him to pray for me because of heart palpitations and all seemingly after this bloody vaccination.

That was all I had spoken of at that moment. Since I came to know PK, he was not only a strong man of faith with so much wisdom and knowledge but also prophetically gifted. I will never forget what I witnessed in the presence of this man, his gifts to others, and his downloads.

PK said, "Glenn, firstly, I know that you are fine because you are protected."

Secondly, he said something so unusual.

ONE MAN'S MISSION TO REDEFINE IMPERFECTION

"You know, I keep hearing about people being vaccinated and having tight chests, but then having been suddenly shocked or electrocuted out of the blue, to only say they have never felt better. Even getting tests done to confirm all is well and the results are fine."

I honestly could not believe what he had just said. He was not even aware of what fully had just happened to me!

As you have read pretty far into my story, you may be blown away to see that my journey appears to have been orchestrated from the start with the Imperfectly Perfect Campaign and mission placed on my heart quite literally.

I have encountered synchronicities and alignments. Experiences like this and so many others I shared earlier clearly show that I am being guided and safeguarded by a force beyond my own to continue my efforts.

Before I knew it, Hollywood movie stars like Dominic Purcell and the Hollywood cast members of Baywatch were posting about the Imperfectly Perfect Campaign, which led to a surge, even more so in the USA.

Just like in Australia, when Rebecca Gibney and Grant Denyer stepped forward, there was a sense of even more credibility behind me and the Imperfectly Perfect Campaign when more prominent names in America came on board.

IMPERFECTLY PERFECT CAMPAIGN

At the same time, I was receiving emails from more networks in Los Angeles that began asking for interviews due to the enormous number of public figures in America who were getting attached to it.

So, a second year, I thought, let me take the chance and head back to the USA.

I took a few weeks out of work—I was still in the construction phase at this point in time—and set my sights back on the bright lights of Hollywood.

The trip blew my mind more than the first trip for many reasons. More and more spontaneity was occurring, doors began to open out of the blue, and lessons were still being learned!

I mean, it is my journey, right?

I would be worried if it was smooth sailing from here on out.

A lesson I learned from being asked on several networks taught me a lot about dealing with media, i.e., producers on shows and their intentions. You see, when I got asked to be on shows in the USA due to my experience with a particular network in Australia, I always asked which celebrity they would like me to bring on.

I took that as usual, but repeatedly, I was met with confusion from producers across separate networks wanting to know why I had asked that.

ONE MAN'S MISSION TO REDEFINE IMPERFECTION

From my experience in Australia, I mentioned that one network always asked me to bring a celebrity on, so I presumed that was normal. I was quickly told it was not and that they were only interested in me here.

The person who created the Imperfectly Perfect Campaign brought these public figures together to make a change.

So yes, a short lesson there and thoughts going around in my head of; "Was this one particular network seeing me as a show 'booker' for them? Let us ask Glenn, and that way, we can bypass management teams or bypass if a celebrity has a fee?"

What a great lesson to learn, though. It only paved the way for me to deal with and navigate conversations with networks and producers in the future. And yes, the lesson was put to effective use further in my story with the same network that I tried before. Just wait.

The trip proved successful for the efforts in the USA. It came as an opportunity for doors to open into Asia and the UK, which I will share further in my journey.

On that trip, I networked with so many people, and through it all, I met people from all around the world who were living in Hollywood for work. This paved the way for introducing the Imperfectly Perfect Campaign and its efforts to them, getting them involved, and sharing it across their networks in countries they were from and were highly regarded and known for their profession.

On this trip, I also learned a lot more about the entertainment industry from a friend who wanted to introduce me in to seeing how it all worked. It was the first time I was invited to several premieres, Q&As, and even Emmy events, which proved to be several comical experiences for me.

The first one.

I stood in the middle of a room with my friends and their acquaintances, networking amongst public figures, producers, casting directors, directors, you name it. Suddenly, I clocked a man looking directly at me across the room. He started shouting and waving in what looked even more in my direction.

Like anybody would, I start looking past me as if to see who he could have possibly been waving at. I mean, nobody knew me. Had he realised that I was nobody and would throw me out?

He suddenly made a beeline to me and said, "Wow, what are you doing here?" I wondered, in my head, what this man was going on about.

Suddenly, he said, 'Oh, you're not him.' My friend latches on and says who? The man responds, 'Oh, I thought you were Simon Peg.'

The laughter filled the air.

ONE MAN'S MISSION TO REDEFINE IMPERFECTION

Now I also laugh here because it was not the first time, I had heard that and sure it will not be the last. It gave for an exceptional story, though, right?

The second comical experience happened at another Emmy event. Many of the biggest reality stars were in attendance, and my friend showed me how the industry worked within casting, demonstrating how they all networked. It was all so fast for me.

People were encircling the stars, business cards were going everywhere, and there was a lot of noise. After a short while, we moved to the side of the room, and my friend, whom I will never forget, said, "Now it's your turn. Go and network."

Because the room was full and I was not enjoying the experience I was seeing, only because it did not feel natural to me. I said hesitantly, Ok I will do it. I disappeared straight to the bar, which was out of my friend's sight.

I did not know where to start. I grabbed a bottle of water and stood scanning the room. I saw one man standing alone and decided to speak to him.

I walked up to him and simply said, "How do you come to these events and network like this?"

"Everybody everywhere, I can't hear myself."

He laughed and said he did not really enjoy events like this, but he was the lead guitarist in the band. We got talking about everything but networking and business. I, being from Australia, travel, his music, and the next minute.

A woman walked over to us both, who I instantly recognised as the 'singer' of the evening and star winner of American Idol.

She introduced herself as the man's fiancé.

Then it was only a matter of minutes before several other stars in attendance joined us, including two of Hollywood's most prominent fashion designers, hosts from Queer Eye of the Straight Guy, Ru Paul's Drag Show, and several more stars from American Idol, whom all went on to get behind the Imperfectly Perfect Campaign's efforts.

How comical. I even shocked my friend when I explained later how it all had transpired.

But that is not all that happened on this trip.

God, Glenn. Where does this stop, I bet some of you are thinking.

Who was to know that something I told you about earlier in terms of the channelling session with Eden and Kim would come to fruition at this time. Like what had happened with Jeremy, how I had spontaneously come across him on social media.

One day, I was at the gym and merely opened my Instagram account. Somehow a lady's post was the first on my screen. I was not following her, nor did I recognize her, but I read a post she had

ONE MAN'S MISSION TO REDEFINE IMPERFECTION

written that had been put on my path. It was so vulnerable, so raw, and so honest. It spoke to the true nature of suicide and mental health.

Like with Jeremy, something told me to contact this lady. Once more, it took only a few hours to hear back from her. Her name was Leticia Frye, and we spoke about that post. She shared her story. She listened to what I was doing in the USA. And I will never forget her saying,

'Sign me up. I want to help.'

The next minute, she told me she was going to book flights from Arizona to LA to get involved. And boy, was she somebody who walked the walk. Because she did just that and flew in two days later.

We spent an afternoon shooting for the campaign and filming parts of her story. Then we enjoyed lunch, where she met my family. Before leaving, she turned to me and said something that still gets my hair standing on the back of my arms.

'I think you should contact a friend of mine. I am not sure she will get back to you because of who she is, but she lost her husband to suicide, who is well known worldwide. But here is her number, and you can try.'

IMPERFECTLY PERFECT CAMPAIGN

She wrote a name and number into my phone, and when she handed it back to me, I was gobsmacked. Talinda Bennington, it read.

I said, "Can I ask if Talinda was married to Chester Bennington?"

Leticia said yes and asked why I had asked, "OMG, you will not believe this."

I told her about my channelled session with Eden and Kim and how Chester Bennington had come through, saying he was pushing the Imperfectly Perfect Campaign's efforts. We both had goosebumps come over our bodies.

Eden had told me in the session that I would be shown evidence to prove he was there, and wow, he did not fail to.

You know, I never managed to get through to Talinda. Still, I look back fondly, thinking maybe I was never meant to and that this encounter with Leticia was evidence Chester was like Eden had said; in fact, there was proof that my efforts were being divinely guided.

ONE MAN'S MISSION TO REDEFINE IMPERFECTION
THE MOMENT OF REVELATION

As I have shared numerous experiences, revealing the immense strides the Imperfectly Perfect Campaign was making, it might beg the question:

Did I not seek help or gather a team? Well, let me assure you, I did.

Over the second year and into the third, I enlisted many individuals who eagerly stepped forward to help. However, alongside the naivety that I had finally broken through, another part of my journey seemed to be sent to teach me a number of invaluable lessons.

When I admitted my lack of experience doing something like the Imperfectly Perfect Campaign before, it was not an exaggeration. Let alone bringing people on to something that had grown substantially bigger than I could handle.

There were times when I was inundated by people with good hearts wanting to help my efforts, which was great on the one hand. However, as I was not yet skilled in the art of fine-tuning my discernment in building the right teams, I found myself often

IMPERFECTLY PERFECT CAMPAIGN

bringing people on, hearing many give a good talk about what they could do, only to discover not long afterward that many lacked the expertise in which they said they had or they spoke too much without putting in the application to get anything behind the scenes actually done.

I know a big part of why I brought so many of these people on who had reached out. Besides many being able to talk a good talk, in all honesty, knowing that often, my journey was a solitary journey; let's face it, spending 12-hour days at construction sites, barely seeing my family, and burning the midnight oil to keep things moving, I was lonely. So, when people showed an interest in wanting to help me, I was clearly drawn in and sold.

I was sold into thinking they could not only do the job they had said they could do but also sold because I thought it may relieve some of my loneliness and alleviate some of the burdens I often dealt with.

However, it was a mistake because many times over, it meant I ended up shouldering most of the workload. Despite many people I brought on board having that good talk, and I do know good intentions, progress was often stalled, leaving me to constantly question myself.

Because I did not have the funds to offer compensation back then. Although people never asked and had stepped forward to

ONE MAN'S MISSION TO REDEFINE IMPERFECTION

volunteer, I still felt obliged to pour into those who purported to assist so that I knew I could help them even when things were not moving from their side.

I featured people on podcasts, highlighted their efforts, introduced them to celebrities, and shared my skills in how I was able to get things moving like I had. Yet, the irony was that a pattern kept showing from many of the people I brought in; things just failed to materialise from others.

Let me just say that I am not here to cast judgement on anyone but to merely acknowledge my own shortcomings. Just as I learned to recognise when people were taking advantage of me, in the earlier experiences dealing with my naivety. Now, I found myself grappling with another challenge: discerning the right people to bring to the team with expertise in the areas that needed working on.

Right then, I was not doing an excellent job at it.

With the Imperfectly Perfect Campaign's increasing visibility, you can imagine how many individuals expressed interest in "helping" and how many people often sidetracked me with looking good on paper and giving an amazing talk. Some claimed expertise in networking or celebrity outreach. Yet, month after month, little progress was made unless I took matters into my own hands.

IMPERFECTLY PERFECT CAMPAIGN

Others boasted about their prowess in securing sponsorships yet failed to generate tangible results. Then, some said they were experienced in marketing but seemed to enjoy basking in the spotlight, sharing press coverage that I was bringing in, and garnering praise by sharing the coverage on their platforms.

Yes, I attempted to delegate, but I struggled in the beginning.

I brought people on and put them into the 'friend' zone more than anything, which was, as I learned, not the best thing to do.

ONE MAN'S MISSION TO REDEFINE IMPERFECTION
THE POWER OF SERENDIPITY

So, it is apparent that I made more than my fair share of missteps in so many areas of the Imperfectly Perfect Campaign, right?

Now, particularly so in assembling the right team.

While it is easy to point fingers and label individuals as the "wrong" fit, the truth is more nuanced.

It was again a period of learning about me and the intricacies of leadership and finding the right people for the right reasons. I had mentioned earlier in my story the question put forth to me,

'Are you ready yet' Remember?

This question resounded in my head at this time more than ever.

I grappled with the question so much here, and once again, I would be lying if I said I was not hard on myself, feeling like an idiot and thinking to myself often, 'Was this ever going to go anywhere?'

I mean, not only have I been used and looked over and through, but now I cannot seem to pick the right people to help me move the Imperfectly Perfect Campaign forward in the direction that was mapped out and put before many.

IMPERFECTLY PERFECT CAMPAIGN

Constant questioning myself.

Was I indeed prepared to lead a team, especially without prior experience in such a role? Would I ever be ready? Let's face it: we all have egos, right?

In the beginning, that clouded my judgement, leading me to believe I was probably ready when, in reality, I still had much to learn. And it is perhaps the main factor I attracted the wrong people at the time who simply weren't in alignment and no doubt sent to me to show me that.

Again, right here, I will always give testimony to the right people who were brought along my path at this moment, too.

I have come to realise that those people brought into our lives at these pivotal points are usually brought in unexpectedly to help when things show up that we do not fully know how to deal with.

During this time, one such person came unexpectedly for me and proved an invaluable help in a situation I had not seen coming at all.

And quite frankly, had no idea how to deal with.

The experience I speak of involved a musician who had expressed interest in contributing a song to the campaign from overseas. Despite my repeated assurances that a song was not needed, they continued crafting one.

ONE MAN'S MISSION TO REDEFINE IMPERFECTION

When I received a text message one morning accompanied by a completed song, I was caught off guard after consistently saying one was not needed.

Thankfully, I had the foresight to seek guidance from the person I mentioned, who came to me unexpectedly at this time and who just happened to be well-versed in entertainment law as a profession.

Their intervention proved invaluable, as they swiftly uncovered discrepancies when talking over conversations with the musician who had sent an accompanying email that listed a set of 'collaborative' details with providing a song (that was not asked or needed), including:

- Having the musician appear on networks with the Imperfectly Perfect Campaign.
- Head to the USA when the Imperfectly Perfect Campaign returns and have the song roll out as the official theme song for the Imperfectly Perfect Campaign.

The person who kindly assisted me with this experience halted any further conversations within a day.

This experience served as a stark reminder of the importance of more discernment with caution, especially as the Imperfectly Perfect Campaign continued to gain traction on an international level.

IMPERFECTLY PERFECT CAMPAIGN

It underscored that as the Imperfectly Perfect Campaign ascended to new heights, I would encounter more individuals who may not have my best interests at heart. That may attempt to play games or assert their supposed superiority, given their 'industry' experience.

Moreover, it also highlighted the need for a mediator capable of impartially assessing situations and safeguarding against emotional manipulation.

In this instance, having a middle person allowed for a clearer perspective and prevented undue influence from clouding my judgement. This episode served as yet another lesson.

… And I know, right!!!

Lesson after lesson after lesson.

Can you imagine how many times I cried out for a breakthrough?

I knew they were for my own good, and this one—well, it reinforced the adage that with new levels of achievement come new challenges and adversaries.

As I continued to navigate the complexities of leadership, I was reminded of the importance of surrounding myself with the right people while maintaining a vigilant eye for hidden agendas, even more so.

ONE MAN'S MISSION TO REDEFINE IMPERFECTION

IMPERFECTLY PERFECT CAMPAIGN
REMEMBERING MICHAEL FALZON

Losing someone special is never easy. Their absence leaves a void that cannot be filled, their memory forever etched in our hearts. Michael Falzon was one of those unique individuals who left an indelible mark on my life, and his passing shook me to the core.

I had spoken earlier in my story about the remarkable people brought into my life, and Michael was undoubtedly one of them. His spirit, his passion, and his unwavering positivity were infectious, lighting up every room he entered.

As I mentioned earlier in my story, in July 2019, Michael called me out of the blue to ask if he could head over to the studio with me in the coming days to record some news he had to share. As the day rolled around, Michael turned up, gave me the biggest hug, and said thank you for this. The funny thing was, I had no idea what news he was about to share.

We set up the camera, and Michael went live to share the news about his sudden diagnosis of a rare form of cancer. I kept filming but was in total disbelief. Despite facing such a daunting challenge,

ONE MAN'S MISSION TO REDEFINE IMPERFECTION

Michael approached it with remarkable courage and resilience. He was determined to fight; he was in high spirits and had said that the good news was that they had caught it early.

Not only was the news something that blew me away that day, but the sheer fact that, at a time, many would recoil with their loved ones and be coming to terms with what this all meant, Michael thought about everybody else. He thought about being of service to others to share his personal news with the world.

There are still no words as to how selfless this man was.

On the morning of 23 June 2020, while at the gym, I received a message from Michelle Stephenson, who had shot a podcast episode alongside Michael and me. The words in her message cut through me like a knife: "We've lost Michael."

The news hit me like a train for someone I had not known for long. As I sit here, a tear rolls down my cheek that I can feel, and I gaze at a picture of Michael I still have on my office desk as I write, recalling that day. My eyes filled up there, and then, I had honestly never experienced such a sense of grief before. It is hard to explain why I felt so emotional.

As I mentioned, I had not known Michael for that long in the grand scheme of things, but the connection I felt towards him upon hearing the news broke me. I had to leave the gym promptly, masking the tears as I passed by others to the exit. Then, the tears just flowed.

I remember the day because of the news and something profound that happened. As I was walking, visibly upset, I remembered it was a stunning day—blue skies, no clouds, and no wind.

I tell you this because something caught my eye without any explanation as to why something could happen that did.

Unexpectedly, a single white feather gently glided towards me in one split second, not just passing by but straight towards my direction. Clear blue skies, no clouds, no wind, no birds flying above me (for those cynical people), just a profound stillness in the air.

I will always remember the feather because there is a later importance to this, which I will soon share. At the time, do not ask me how or why—I just knew that it was a sign that Michael was around me at that moment.

A month later, I received an unexpected message. This time from Michael's wife, Jane. Now, I had only met Jane once before at an event Michael had extended an invitation to me, albeit briefly, so I was not aware that Jane knew much about me.

However, her message was a touching surprise as she shared that Michael had frequently spoken fondly of me and felt led to extend

ONE MAN'S MISSION TO REDEFINE IMPERFECTION

a heartfelt invitation to his private funeral service. I was deeply moved by this gesture, realising that Michael had clearly expressed me in high regard for Jane to consider me for such an intimate occasion.

In fact, it took me back; I was touched.

Michael was not just anybody; like I had said, he was Australian Musical Royalty; everybody knew Michael; he had played the big international stages, sang alongside some of the world's greats, and hadn't known me half as long as many others. Still, it meant a lot that he spoke fondly of me, enough for Jane to invite me, let alone even remember me with every emotion she would have been going through.

The day of the service arrived, and despite the sombre occasion, it was a celebration of Michael's extraordinary life. As tributes poured in from Australia's legendary artists and musicians, we were all reminded of Michael's profound impact on everyone he encountered.

His humility, generosity, and boundless love touched the lives of all who knew him. As tears flowed freely in the room, I could not help but reflect on Michael's lessons about living with grace, kindness, and gratitude and what it meant to leave a lasting legacy that would continue to live on, even through his passing.

IMPERFECTLY PERFECT CAMPAIGN

Though Michael may no longer be with us in body, his spirit lives on in the countless lives he touched and in the Imperfectly Perfect Campaign.

Rest in peace, dear friend. You will be forever missed but never forgotten.

ONE MAN'S MISSION TO REDEFINE IMPERFECTION
THE TRUE COST BEHIND FREE RESOURCES

As I had previously mentioned, to get the Imperfectly Perfect Campaign through the pandemic and keep people connected, alongside working full-time, I was still focused on maintaining connections.

I had moved forward by commencing the Podcast, Community Initiatives, and 'Virtual Hangs' to keep people connected. All of which, were offered for free.

The events were designed to be a lifeline of connection, featuring guests sharing their stories, talents, and expertise. From celebrities to practitioners, the virtual hangs became a sanctuary for many seeking solace and community.

But as they grew, so did the costs. Once more, I found that if I was to continue this on a larger scale, the costs would accrue, and it would be on me to cover them. The minimal revenue from apparel sales simply could not cover much.

IMPERFECTLY PERFECT CAMPAIGN

Recognising I could no longer sustain this, I introduced a nominal fee for future events to ensure more sustainability and value for all involved. Given that some people were not working at the time, I set a minimal fee of only ten dollars to cover hosting platforms and marketing efforts.

However, what unfolded next was a sobering revelation.

A friend alerted me to whispers from within the community, suggesting that I had somehow changed, becoming more focused on profit than purpose. It was a gut punch of disbelief and indignation. How could someone misconstrue my actions as anything other than a necessary step towards sustainability?

In the aftermath, I grappled with a harsh truth: I had unwittingly cultivated a culture of expectation where my generosity was taken for granted. The realisation was a bitter pill to swallow, forcing me to confront my own boundaries and reassess my approach to philanthropy and community.

The period that followed was one of deep introspection. I pressed pause on all the events, turning inward to understand how I had arrived at this juncture. This period also revealed another important lesson—yes, another one!

Through the free events, I observed a pattern emerging. Upon discovering our free events, specific individuals attempted to take advantage of the opportunity for personal gain.

ONE MAN'S MISSION TO REDEFINE IMPERFECTION

A particular publicist attended our gatherings on two occasions, seeking connections. During one event featuring a prominent Hollywood figure, they brought along a colleague and openly attempted to pitch their own project. To my surprise, the celebrity guest graciously redirected them, emphasising that the events were not platforms for self-promotion.

All this freely giving to a community led to the stark realisation that my altruism had inadvertently become a double-edged sword.

In my eagerness to give, I had also needed to establish firm boundaries within the community I had built. In pursuing connection and wanting to keep people connected, I overlooked the importance of self-preservation.

It was a hard-won lesson, but once again, it helped me understand the need to keep going.

Let's face it, I wasn't going to give up now!

So, in the wake of misplaced expectations, I resolved to forge a new path—one characterised by balance, discernment, and an unyielding commitment to self-preservation.

Despite transparency throughout my journey to clarify that the Imperfectly Perfect Campaign received no external funding, if some people did not appreciate my endeavours or see what it took behind the scenes, I realised there was little I could do about it.

IMPERFECTLY PERFECT CAMPAIGN

Worrying about others' perceptions or fearing judgement proved futile. After all, money in the hands of those with noble intentions can achieve remarkable feats. If a few voices criticised me without actively contributing to positive change, I resolved to let their opinions slide.

ONE MAN'S MISSION TO REDEFINE IMPERFECTION
SCREW THIS!

I could sit here right now and tell you that every single one of these lessons seemed relentless. Yet they were all pushing me forward and building my resilience, faith, discernment, and more to develop who I needed to become. Although lessons are relentless, they will always attest to you questioning yourself occasionally. We are all human.

On the one hand, I was getting confirmation that the Imperfectly Perfect Campaign was being divinely led, seemingly doing the right things, not going down the conventional routes which my intuition kept telling me to avoid. Yet, at another time, another relentless lesson. I wanted to say screw this.

The physical aspect of showing up each day into another year of what I felt was going around in circles had gotten to me. Think about it. Because my mind, indeed, was at this point.

It was after all of the relentless past experiences—the pandemic, which continued to halt the world, finishing up with the non-profit organisation, continually trying to keep people connected, trying to find ways to fund everything, an individual questioning my ethics, and, on top of trying to take care of my family—that I finally hit a wall.

The lessons were making me grow, sure.

But the application of putting in the work across everything seemed futile at this point. At the time, I saw myself continually giving out and nothing coming in for me. No breakthrough. No work due to covid. The fear of where or what I would do next floored me.

Thankfully, my family was okay financially. Still, nonetheless, for a few months, nothing came in from my side once mine started dwindling. I remember heading into the bathroom, closing the door, hearing my wife and kids playing, and thinking to myself, how am I supposed to contribute to this right now?

If it was not for having savings and my wife still working, then what?

I was harsh on myself. Everyone was telling me what I was doing was being led by divine forces, and honestly, I started questioning it all.

Prove it.

Here I am, giving my all for everybody else, trying my best, and now, I am struggling. I am exhausted. I am both physically and mentally drained.

ONE MAN'S MISSION TO REDEFINE IMPERFECTION

It seemed like no matter what I did or how hard I tried, even with boundaries and seeing through people, there were still tests coming thick and fast to see if I had learned! I had, and I was genuinely starting to get over it all.

Some of me felt invisible, as if my efforts did not matter and that my worth was insignificant to others.

I had connected with and brought people along to things related to my work, for introductions and, more so, doing things and bringing people along projects, even those I had connected them to, forgetting Glenn.

People were still flocking to me for connections to celebrities I know, and so-called friends constantly picked my brain for advice on PR and Marketing, disguised as flattery.

'But Glenn, I just respect your advice.'

I found myself grappling with the psychology of it all. Why was I feeling like this now, after all the lessons I had gone through and thought I was doing good? Why did I continue attracting people who did not value me or my contributions?

Why did I allow myself to be treated as less than I deserved?

I am not saying that something suddenly clicked because it took a couple of weeks of being hard on myself to realise something.

I did not respect myself, my worth, or the hard work I had put in, so how could others? I was sending out signals of self-doubt and

IMPERFECTLY PERFECT CAMPAIGN

insecurity, and the universe responded by sending me more of the same.

ONE MAN'S MISSION TO REDEFINE IMPERFECTION
REDEFINING WHAT COMES NEXT

My story takes a turn here—and for the better!

I reckon you are even reading this and thinking, thank God, right!

By gaining clarity about the respect, I lacked in myself, I made the conscious decision to take a break and step back from the Imperfectly Perfect Campaign, allowing myself the opportunity to delve deeper into introspection. Not quit—I had come too far—but merely take a break and step back.

I aimed to unravel the layers of each experience that had been presented to me up until this point, particularly those highlighting instances of self-respect deficiency, and understand their origins more profoundly.

I also took the time to avoid spiralling down a path of self-destructiveness dictated by my own perceptions, succumbing to cynicism toward people and their actions, or adopting a victim mentality toward myself.

While I never considered myself to harbour a negative mindset, my experiences had clearly influenced my thoughts at times. As I had mentioned earlier, I found myself sometimes berating my actions.

Labelling myself as foolish for allowing specific experiences to linger.

Through that journey, I embarked on a profound exploration of self-discovery. Delving into the depths of my being, I confronted the shadows that obscured the very sense of my self-respect. With each revelation, I embraced the mantle of responsibility, recognising its pivotal role in shaping my path. I understood that nurturing self-respect was more paramount to my personal growth than I had known.

I resolved to transform my thoughts, habits, and inner dialogue, which, if I had continued, could have become self-destructive to me and to my efforts.

This period was not without its trials. I grappled with past traumas and buried emotions that I never knew I had carried around with me.

As I frequently remark, the journey of inner work, spiritual exploration, or faith is not all rainbows and butterflies.

If somebody tells you it is, I say run!

It led me through confrontations with fears I had not realised I had, into the shadows of my psyche, and through emotional depths I never imagined existed. It compelled me to confront

ONE MAN'S MISSION TO REDEFINE IMPERFECTION

uncomfortable areas I had not realised I held on to and embrace even more honesty in every facet of my being.

It required dedication, perseverance, and hard work to move through all those core beliefs I held beyond old traumas and unexpressed emotions that controlled me.

But beyond it all, the rewards were immeasurable.

I came out of it having discovered moments of profound catharsis, renewal, and profound truths about myself.

And I will say to anybody.

An experience like that leaves an indelible mark. One that you will never forget. It is like unlocking a hidden reservoir of inner strength, a toolkit that assures you can weather any storm life throws.

It is often said that we can only truly connect with others to the extent that we have explored within ourselves, and I've found this to be profoundly true.

Going more profound than I had ever before, the Imperfectly Perfect Campaign did not just need somebody at the helm to address awareness of the problem but also to be a part of the solution in helping others move forward and heal too. So, as much as the inner work was hard, it became a profound gift of self-discovery that I needed.

IMPERFECTLY PERFECT CAMPAIGN

I needed to see myself with the self-assurance, self-respect, and self-worth that God clearly had seen in me to know I was the right person for the mission. I needed to be the person to lead from the front, even more so now, as a beacon of hope for those struggling and trapped in cycles of suffering, and to extend a guiding hand myself.

Not only to bring awareness to the surface but also to encourage and force a solution for others to embark on their own journey of self-discovery and healing.

ONE MAN'S MISSION TO REDEFINE IMPERFECTION
INNER WORK, OUTER STRENGTH

This period of inner work I had embarked on was paramount for me. As we slowly emerged from the shadow of a global pandemic, I knew that these past couple of years had armed me with the insights that I was ready to navigate any challenges ahead and continue to make a positive impact.

It was a moment to shine, inspire, and be a force for good in the world and let people know who Glenn was.

I have touched upon this notion before, but it's worth reminding people. What tends to happen when you start the work on yourself is more tests. The universe seems to send forth new experiences to almost assess your newfound knowledge and insights and see if you have truly learned from them. Plus, see if you are ready to face the areas you needed to confront.

And boy, was I put to the test again!

This time, it came from an international organisation looking to expand into the Australian market, which reached out to me. Their outreach to discuss potential collaborations clearly indicated that

IMPERFECTLY PERFECT CAMPAIGN

my work was gaining even more significant recognition on a larger scale.

Now, I was being placed in front of multi-million-dollar entities.

It was both exhilarating and humbling to see the impact of my efforts and the doors they opened. But beyond the excitement, I could not ignore the more profound significance of this encounter.

It felt like the universe was presenting me with a monumental test of the lessons I had learned, particularly those centred around respect for what was to transpire. This was not just a small-scale trial; it was a colossal challenge, one that would truly test my newfound wisdom and self-respect.

I was invited to a meeting, where I found myself face-to-face with the CEO and several executives who had reached out to me to see how we could work together. The organisation was driving its efforts into the Australian market in a space similar to the Imperfectly Perfect Campaign, so they saw ample opportunity to come together somehow, they had said.

As we conversed, I learned about their endeavours towards mental well-being, and they expressed interest in learning more about the Imperfectly Perfect Campaign and my achievements.

To cut to the chase, their vision seemed to involve integrating several of their executives and well-being experts as guests on the Imperfectly Perfect Campaign's platform to highlight and discuss

ONE MAN'S MISSION TO REDEFINE IMPERFECTION

their work. While they seemed enthusiastic about this idea, my mind was focused on the work I had been doing on myself, particularly regarding respect. I realised I had nothing to lose; they had approached me.

I was not about to let myself down here. So, I spoke up.

I addressed their proposal very professionally but began questioning them about how bringing their team onto my platform would benefit my endeavours. As it would seem, I could only see how it would benefit them rather than me.

Then, I outlined a mutually beneficial scenario.

I would bring them onto my platform to share their mental health and well-being work. They could contribute to my global efforts as an official sponsor for the Imperfectly Perfect Campaign. Given their entry into the Australian market, I would serve as an official speaker at their upcoming event to discuss the Imperfectly Perfect Campaign and my efforts.

After all, they had contacted me, wanting to work together somehow. It was a win-win proposition that aligned with both of our goals.

They requested a proposal for consideration, and after the meeting concluded, I was now challenged to create one…for a multi-million-dollar organisation. Despite never tackling such a

IMPERFECTLY PERFECT CAMPAIGN

task before, I dedicated myself to learning the intricacies of business proposals.

With relentless effort, I crafted a comprehensive proposal outlining the details of the Imperfectly Perfect Campaign's offering and how becoming an official sponsor could benefit them, emphasising the return on investment.

With the inner work I had been doing on myself regarding self-respect, there was no way I would drop the ball and be seen as a free resource for any person or company ever again. Let's look at this logically. A multi-million-dollar organisation approaches me.

And with no doubt in my mind that they would already be paying tens of thousands of dollars in marketing efforts for their organisation and what they were wanting to bring towards the Australian Market. They are reaching out to me and want me to feature their work through their well-being experts and executives on my international platform for free.

Sorry, not a chance.

They could look elsewhere if they were not willing to partner in a way that benefited everybody.

Low and behold, weeks and months passed without a response. This told me all I needed to know.

I had forgotten about them, honestly, due to the amount of time that had passed over the next several months or so. However, just

ONE MAN'S MISSION TO REDEFINE IMPERFECTION

two months before their planned visit to Australia, I received an email from a new member of their team wanting to touch base.

At the meeting they set up, I was surprised to be greeted by this 'new' team member I had not previously encountered. Not the CEO or any of the executives I had met previously. Odd, I thought.

This 'new' team member initiated the conversation, under the impression that the previous discussion revolved around coordinating executives and well-being experts as guests on my show and getting them locked in. That clearly was not the case, nor was it ever going to be.

Politely but firmly, I redirected the person to go back and clarify the purpose of the previous meeting with the CEO and executives who had been present.

Also, respectfully, I told them to mention that if the following conversation did not address their organisation as official sponsors for the Imperfectly Perfect Campaign or my role as a speaker at their launch event, I was not interested. I never did hear back.

However, I was not disheartened. With all the work I had just done on myself, I remained confident in my abilities, knowing my worth and the value I brought.

I understood precisely why they were interested in collaborating with me, and their lack of response did not diminish that. Still furthermore, it propelled a deeper knowledge of my worth.

IMPERFECTLY PERFECT CAMPAIGN

If multi-million-dollar organisations were reaching out to me, it became evident that they saw value in what I could offer to their endeavours, whether it was generating publicity, leveraging my extensive global connections, or using my skills to get attention.

For this reason, I chose to express gratitude to them. Their interest served as a powerful reminder of my worth and capabilities. Unbeknownst to them, they had taught me to recognise and appreciate the unique strengths I brought to the table, how to hold my own and respect that my time and efforts be appreciated, and that I was worth being equally poured into as well. For that, I will always be thankful.

Suppose you are venturing into making a difference, starting a company, or any endeavour that demands courage and determination. In that case, you will see through my journey that you will face every possible test.

How you handle these tests determines your path forward. That is why I urge you to prioritise self-work. Strengthen your discernment, resilience, confidence, and, most importantly, your self-worth and self-respect.

These qualities will guide you through the inevitable challenges you will encounter.

ONE MAN'S MISSION TO REDEFINE IMPERFECTION
IN THE PRESENCE OF THE DIVINE

I have shared extensively about my journey of seeking, exploring, and delving into the depths of spirituality and faith. Despite never identifying as religious or claiming to have any profound knowledge about God, you have read that I have often found myself turning to a higher power in moments of need and questioning.

Yet, it was not until a pivotal moment that I genuinely felt a connection with God. One night, as I slept, I woke in the morning with the word "baptism" lingering in my mind. Dreams are rare for me, and recalling one, let alone extracting a specific word, felt peculiar.

Nonetheless, the word persisted enough for me to share it with my wife. What happened next seemed too coincidental to ignore. That morning, as I logged onto social media to post content for the Imperfectly Perfect Campaign, a friend's post caught my eye.

"Does anybody want to come to church with me?" the post read.

It was a proposition I had never considered before. Yet, that intuitive nudge of mine reared its head and prompted me to

IMPERFECTLY PERFECT CAMPAIGN

message my friend. With the stereotypical image of a British stoic church in mind, I tentatively enquired about the nature of his church.

His response was unexpected: "It's full of families, young people, live music, worship—just come and see for yourself."

It was a far cry from what I had imagined, and with curiosity piqued, I felt compelled to experience it firsthand. So, as my friend had suggested, I took the leap and attended the Sunday evening service at 5:30 p.m.

As I walked in, I was pleasantly surprised to see that he was not exaggerating—it indeed was a diverse group of young people, families, and the elderly gathered together. Live music filled the air, and I could not help but feel a sense of openness and inclusivity.

However, it could be overwhelming if this is the first time you have experienced such an atmosphere. As we entered the service, the music and worship continued, with people enthusiastically lifting their hands up in the air and worshipping. Meanwhile, I stood still, lost in my thoughts, trying to understand it all. I looked around at everybody with their hands in the air and thought, "I hope nobody is expecting me to do that."

As the music gradually faded, the lead pastor stepped onto the stage to speak, followed by others who stood up and shared personal stories. What captivated me was their willingness to share their imperfections, struggles, and the paths they had walked that had not served them well.

It was very different from the formal, scripted church services I had seen depicted on TV or attended for christenings and weddings back in the UK. They spoke of addictions, feelings of loneliness, depression, tough times, and more. It was moving to witness people in a church talk so openly, so unfiltered, raw, and honest, and be shown love by everybody in the room.

But it was what happened next that left me utterly stunned. The lead pastor then went on to draw a conclusion to the service. He began to discuss the upcoming month, emphasising the significance of baptisms—water baptisms, to be exact. It felt like a bolt from the blue. I mean, seriously!

Only a few days earlier, I had woken up with the word "baptism" on my mind. Then, the following day, a friend posted about going to church. And now, here I was, hearing them speak about baptisms at the service. My logical mind tried to rationalise it, assuming they must have baptisms regularly. Yet, to my surprise, I learned that they only conducted water baptisms every six months. Its synchronicity left me awestruck.

Once more, it served as a reminder and made unmistakably clear that my event, experience, and step were part of that meticulously orchestrated plan. I believed. I had no reason anymore not to think

IMPERFECTLY PERFECT CAMPAIGN

or have complete faith that what was happening for me was part of something far more significant than me. Everything was showing me signs and becoming increasingly undeniable.

I can only laugh thinking that 'up there' they must be saying.

'Have we shown you enough yet, Glenn? Have we finally got your attention? Now, do you believe?'

Everything was clearly screaming out signs with such intensity that dismissing them would have been silly. I would have been foolish not to surrender, believe, or have utter faith in it all. And yes, although I had all those things, my question now was, am I being drawn closer to God?

I found myself attending more services and even engaging in meeting up with groups, eagerly learning and listening from them yet still grappling with the profound concepts presented to me. Something I will be honest and say here. Never in a million years did I see myself doing this. It did take time for me to openly acknowledge the presence of God in my life, driven in part by a fear of judgment and a reluctance to be perceived as "religious" by others. Yet, suddenly, I merely came to recognise that my spiritual path was uniquely mine and finally just said 'God' to anybody and everyone.

The opinions of others could not dictate my truth in what I was trying to do in the world with the Imperfectly Perfect Campaign. I

ONE MAN'S MISSION TO REDEFINE IMPERFECTION

had also let go of the fear of judgment on what others thought of me a long time ago, so why would or should I care if somebody thought I'm religious if I said God? I finally embraced the signs pointing me toward God with a newfound conviction. As I grew more in terms of my personal relationship with God, don't let me fool you into thinking I knew it all.

I did not and as much as I was still seeking, friends of faith often laughed when they would say, 'Glenn's waiting for the red carpet to be rolled out and God to walk down to speak to him.'

I often laughed and said, well, is that not how it is supposed to happen? I did not know what I did not know. I heard so many people's 'testimonies' of profound experiences, being spoken to, and speaking in tongues once filled with the Holy Spirit; what was I to honestly believe or think?

Even as I continued walking this newfound path, there were things I was witnessing online and around me that did not sit well with even 'faith.' I think it is safe to say that my intuition and those nudges have served me well throughout everything, right?

Especially when something was off or did not feel right.

Well, once more, what I saw around me regarding some people of 'faith' or 'religion,' if that is what they led by, left me feeling uneasy, like something was off.

IMPERFECTLY PERFECT CAMPAIGN

It was becoming increasingly common to encounter individuals who, upon discovering faith, seemed to have suddenly undergone such radical transformations in their beliefs and behaviours that not only in person but also on social platforms, they would start suddenly preaching like they knew everything and seemed to be dictating what was right or wrong. Even as far as condemning those who did not conform to their way of thinking. I was suddenly seeing emerging narratives screamed out, from fervent proselytising to harsh judgment of others who do not, as I mentioned, conform to those preaching their newfound convictions.

An emergence of individuals who suddenly became self-righteous in their interpretation of teachings, preaching, and condemning those whose lifestyles diverged from their own in the form of public chastisement and online diatribes. I was not judging the person or people; I just found myself questioning their actions and then questioning God for answers as to why many people acting out like this were being 'put in front of' me or were across my social platforms.

You know how that one goes, right?

There is a reason when somebody or something is put on your path to learn something from. I just could not fathom that so many people of faith, despite them sharing their previous lifestyles and experiences prior to their profound awakening, were somehow listening to someone who seemed to have propelled them into the role of moral arbiters.

One truly notable example of somebody who was put in front of me, after embracing faith, transitioned into a vocal preacher of religious doctrine, condemning behaviours such as partying, substance use, and alternative spiritual practices, which was precisely what they were previously known for. While the transformation itself was absolutely amazing in them, and it is in anybody, and trying to speak to people is commendable, the manner in which they had chosen to express their newfound beliefs was just beyond me; my grasp of faith and what God, I thought, was teaching me on my journey. It just felt off to me.

I just felt that if I was back to seeking and came across somebody chastising and judging me on how I lived, without knowing anything about me or the experiences that had shaped me to live that way, it would not give me a source of inspired action to want to learn more about their beliefs or even want me to get to know God.

What I was taking from my relationship with God was to let his work shine through me in my actions. Now, this obviously can be done in whatever way people feel led. Personally, I just knew I did not have to preach the word nor shout it from the rooftops to proclaim that I followed God or had a relationship with him. And I certainly never felt that I had to know everything to claim what was right or wrong. I simply do not know.

After all, I am not perfect, and I certainly would not want to impart any wisdom I've learned from God by dictating how others should walk their journey and telling them that they are wrong when I don't have all the answers myself. I have literally stumbled my way up until this point.

So, I am far from speaking words that sound self-righteous, thinking I could tell others the correct way of life. Yet, clearly, my path has been led, and through it all, what I have been able to do in bringing all the 'imperfect' people together to share their stories to help others heal is something that God is working through me for others to see. Not to judge, not to chastise, not to dictate, and not to tell anybody they are wrong in who they were created to be.

ONE MAN'S MISSION TO REDEFINE IMPERFECTION
QUESTIONING MY FAITH

One thing I started to have a challenging time with towards the church and ideas around religion was what seemed to be a structured set of beliefs. Now, I am not here to impose what anybody else should see in what I say. I am speaking my own truths and am confident that I hold firm to the belief that conforming oneself to any structured system of beliefs dictated by others can be detrimental. This is precisely why I would refuse to label myself as religious because, simply put, I am not.

I remain steadfast in my convictions about God and testify to him daily. However, I would refuse to entertain judgments from anybody claiming that I must conform to what this world or they want me to believe simply because they do. We are each on our unique journey, and it's imperative to navigate it authentically, keep our power, and take what another person says as correct or not.

It may very well be for them, but is it for all of us? I do not know and wouldn't want to preach or dictate if it is. Again, I had previously mentioned things that I had witnessed in new believers suddenly speaking as moral arbiters, and what I was about to have

IMPERFECTLY PERFECT CAMPAIGN

happen to me became a significant driver in why I would never accept the dictates of this world taking what people had to say as gospel, especially not without engaging in genuine seeking, listening, questioning, and intuitive guidance through my own understanding.

However, here we go again.

At one point, early in my attendance at many gatherings, I gradually fell into the trap of beginning to listen too much about the righteous way of living with faith in how people of this world were speaking of it. I started scrutinising my own righteousness and wondering if I were not perfect enough, that it could be what may be hindering certain aspects of the Imperfectly Perfect Campaign's internal progress. I found myself succumbing to the insidious thought that I simply was not righteous enough or that I maybe sinful in some way because, often, that is all you would hear people of faith speak on.

Everything was a sin. This is a sin; that is a sin. You cannot do this; you cannot do that. It sounds crazy to me now, but honestly, I saw myself knowing the feelings of those very people I had witnessed in those networking rooms in the clubhouse I spoke of, listening to those supposed men and women of God telling others that they had to pour dollar amounts into them to receive their blessing. They were seeking, emotionally drained, and did not

ONE MAN'S MISSION TO REDEFINE IMPERFECTION

know what was true, so they took what others said as gospel. In hindsight, I realise how deep a rabbit hole religion can become if one allows it.

Given my inclination to question everything, inconsistencies began to emerge. I was not indoctrinated into religion, which allowed my mind to remain open to continual seeking and learning. I also held true to my commitment to question anything that did not intuitively feel right.

Herein lies the dilemma:

We often witness individuals preaching from positions of authority, condemning certain behaviours as sinful, only to later discover their own moral failings. We hear many new believers condemn others by posting on social media, only to come out later to say that they 'sinned' and asking for forgiveness. We see people of faith condemn and judge, and we have seen them fall short. We have seen and heard of false prophets, those who use the name of God for greed and power. It simply did not add up to me.

Now, I am not here to certainly judge any of those and their apparent shortcomings as many in faith would proclaim them as. But as I delved deeper into introspection, I began to recognise the danger of tethering my worth to an arbitrary standard of righteousness defined by what people told me. It dawned on me that allowing external judgments to dictate my journey stifled my

IMPERFECTLY PERFECT CAMPAIGN

growth and suffocated my sense of self in my relationship with God.

I have mentioned that many men and women of God, friends of mine have joked that Glenn thinks God will walk down a red carpet and speak directly to him. I soon started understanding that God did not necessarily do that but speaks to us in various ways. Through it, other people who are sent on our paths, through words that simply come to mind, through music put across our path, our dreams, and it can be several ways.

A big thing for me was having people put on my path at the right moments when I needed answers. And hey presto, during this time of unsettlement, as I was not feeling quite right about what I was witnessing and had lots of questions. Campbell Johnstone, one of New Zealand's All-Black Professional Rugby Players, was placed on my path.

Unbeknownst to him, he spoke directly into me on an episode of my show and simply confirmed all I had felt that had not been sitting right with me. Albeit a different circumstance, he brought up on the show, unexpectedly, how, due to religion, he had been hiding who he was for such a long time. He felt like each time he wasn't picked for a team or a match, or he didn't play well enough, he was attesting it to being not who he really was, not being

ONE MAN'S MISSION TO REDEFINE IMPERFECTION

'righteous' enough, and being punished to the point that it started becoming detrimental to his mental health.

Until he found himself throwing his hands in the air one day, talking to God, and saying he could not go on like this any longer. He finally accepted himself; he remained steadfast in his conviction in God but let all the harbouring 'religious' dogma that the world put on him go. Guess what, his life turned around, and to this day, he gives testimony to God.

Now, like I said, albeit a different circumstance for myself. It became the same teaching. I had started to feel that I was not perfect enough, that maybe I wasn't doing things the right way, and that was why certain facets of my work didn't seem to be working. This confirmation came when I was going through this stage of feeling that something was off. It was a wake-up call to question where I had allowed myself to be led to this notion.

Just like Campbell had mentioned, throwing his hands up and saying no more. In my own moment of clarity after listening to him speak, I experienced a profound liberation. I realised that my connection with God was not contingent upon adhering to rigid doctrines or conforming to societal expectations. Instead, it was about forging a personal relationship—a direct line of communication between my soul and the divine.

IMPERFECTLY PERFECT CAMPAIGN

At that moment, I let those thoughts that I was not righteous enough simply dissipate. This realisation sparked a newfound freedom within me to explore a relationship with him, guided by my intuition and inner wisdom and not listen to others.

Through connecting with God on a deeply personal level, I found solace, guidance, and a sense of purpose that transcended any external standards or judgments. Oh, and I also got smacked in the face with the notion that here I was, having had my journey clearly orchestrated by being 'imperfect,' and yet I almost allowed myself to conform to being 'perfect.'

Ironic, right?

ONE MAN'S MISSION TO REDEFINE IMPERFECTION
THE MAN YOU MEET TODAY

So, how did I finally say no more to this world? I was no longer content to simply exist; I stopped listening to everyone and everything around me, even towards faith. This was my path, my journey, and as my good friend Rachael loves to say, "We are here to experience this life, so make the most of it." That was what I was going to do from here on out.

I was determined to thrive, to make a meaningful impact, and to leave my mark on the world in my own unique way through my Voice. Now, I was not just making an impact by sharing everybody else's voices but also letting the world know exactly who Glenn Marsden was.

The man who, yes, had the mission placed on his heart, but also the man who had the conviction to make change, to bring together the world's biggest names, the man who single-handedly learned every facet of marketing, public relations, and networking while simultaneously holding down a job and supporting a family, and the man who was willing to make some noise in the world in an area he saw a problem with.

IMPERFECTLY PERFECT CAMPAIGN

I was no longer content with playing small, tiptoeing around my own potential by sharing only others' stories and highlighting the movement's efforts. I was going to go BIG on highlighting who I was.

God had clearly opened my eyes through so many relentless lessons and tests to show me who I was, what I brought to the world, and what difference I was making. With this deep sense of knowing came a surge of confidence coursing through my veins like never before. It was as if my eyes somehow had been opened to understanding exactly why people and these larger organisations were continually seeking my input or trying to 'collaborate.' I saw clearly why people kept turning to me for guidance and assistance.

It was not merely because of my work; it was because (and some would never admit it) they all saw the massive amount of value I brought to the table, the wisdom I had accumulated through my journey, and what I could do for them. A shift in perspective came to me. I began to understand that it was essential to consider what I gained from everything. It was not selfishness; it came back to the self-respect.

It came back to all the years I had worked on building what I had and now had the knowledge and skillset to help others. It came back to knowing that if I wanted to make the Imperfectly Perfect Campaign as successful and global as I had envisioned it to be, it was my turn to step up and be poured into what I could offer to all those coming towards me. I needed to ensure that my own cup was filled, that I was supported and nurtured in return for the energy and expertise I offered, and that people constantly wanted from me.

It was a turning point where I embraced the idea of reciprocity without guilt or hesitation. Yes, I would still be kind and do the work for those I was trying to help through my endeavours with my time and efforts. Still, outside of that, I would no longer be naive to the value of my time and contributions to those reaching out to me and wanting to take from me towards their business endeavours.

I demanded respect, not out of arrogance but of understanding my worth. If somebody wanted my time, skill set, and knowledge, they could pour me so that, in turn, I could continue my philanthropic work with the Imperfectly Perfect Campaign.

At this moment, I also realised the power of my network in connecting people worldwide who had helped me. I was now able to open doors for many people, including public figures, bridging gaps between different countries where they were not predominantly known and who had supported and, indeed, poured into me. It was a humbling experience, showing me how I was now positioned to help those who believed in me, too.

IMPERFECTLY PERFECT CAMPAIGN

It was a reminder of the importance of reciprocity and the interconnectedness of our actions, leading to a more significant collective impact than any individual could achieve alone.

In hindsight, it was also the time. I begged the question, was this the plan all along?

To show me who God saw in me!

To help me understand the importance of me in all of this.

Allowing myself to receive by acknowledging my own needs and my own desires.

Through this new sense, I began creating a feedback loop of abundance that would fuel my mission and amplify its impact as I had envisioned. As we know, I was constantly being steered away from the traditional non-profit model. I now saw that perhaps God used all of this to simply build me up into the person he knew I could be.

In order to make the Imperfectly Perfect Campaign sustainable and take it to heights I could never have imagined unconventionally through ME!

In that moment of questioning, more clarity came to pass. I understood that God's plan was not always obvious or linear. It came with opportunity and challenge, guiding me each step of the way as I have recounted numerous times.

ONE MAN'S MISSION TO REDEFINE IMPERFECTION

I could not help but acknowledge the profound shift that had taken place within me right then and there. The inner work, the introspection, the relentless pursuit of self-improvement, the not-so-nice experiences that I saw as lessons—they had all led me here. I was no longer merely a spectator in what I had created; I was moving forward as an active participant, ready to take on the world with unwavering resolve as I, the founder, the speaker, and the businessman.

Now stood a version of myself that was unapologetically confident, fiercely determined, and acutely aware of the value I brought to the table. As I embraced this newfound sense of empowerment, I found myself attracting opportunities and connections that aligned perfectly with my vision and got poured into at the same time. As I also embraced this truth of what had transpired, I finally felt that I was exactly where I needed to be, doing exactly what I was meant to do, and that was putting ME first to be able to help pour into others who I was trying to help through the Imperfectly Perfect Campaign.

This was, in fact, MY BREAKTHROUGH!

IMPERFECTLY PERFECT CAMPAIGN
REDIRECTING INTENTIONS TOWARD IMPACT

With each person or company that reached out following, seeking, in their words, "collaboration," they encountered a new version of Glenn Marsden – one who was resolute, self-assured, and unapologetically focused on his mission. Gone were the days of entertaining every enquiry my way; now, each meeting was held with a newfound respect for myself and my efforts.

I made it clear from the outset: if they wanted my involvement, they needed to come prepared with concrete proposals outlining how it would benefit both me and my organisation, the Imperfectly Perfect Campaign. If they could not provide satisfactory answers, I politely informed them to return when they had something substantial to offer.

Reflecting on past experiences, like the incident with the musician and the intermediary who intervened on my behalf, I recognised the necessity of establishing clear boundaries by putting people between myself and others. Thus, I decided to hire a

ONE MAN'S MISSION TO REDEFINE IMPERFECTION

personal assistant, someone who could serve as a gatekeeper and direct all enquiries through them.

My bandwidth was limited as it was, and too many were thinking I was accessible and let's face it, nine out of ten times tried to tap into my empathetic side especially if they thought they knew me. That can be a dangerous game. Do not play it!

Moreover, I took a proactive approach in redirecting those seeking my assistance for their agendas. Instead of entertaining their requests, I directed them to book consultations with my Personal Assistant.

This not only freed up my time but also ensured that those who genuinely needed help were given proper attention and consideration. Even when presented with seemingly enticing opportunities, like a network's request to feature Imperfectly Perfect Campaign on their show with two Hollywood names.

I remained steadfast in upholding my standards. This particular network was merely baiting me as a free resource, a show booker as they had done before. I declined immediately when they suggested conducting the interview only with the celebrities. I refused to compromise my principles, being overlooked and the integrity of my mission for the sake of what they wanted and tried to make out that it would interest me. I was no longer willing to be viewed as a free resource available at anyone's disposal.

IMPERFECTLY PERFECT CAMPAIGN

If something did not align with my vision for the Imperfectly Perfect Campaign or serve its greater purpose towards those I was trying to help, I had no qualms about turning it down. After all, I had nothing to lose by prioritising what truly mattered. Nobody regarding those people and organisations that consistently reached out to me, until this point, had thought to be pouring into me or the efforts. Yet, as transparent as I always had been in saying that the Imperfectly Perfect Campaign was not funded or given grants, they would've happily seen me keep pouring out of my pockets while simultaneously having to jump into construction to cover my family and expenses as long as they got what they wanted.

Now, as companies approached me, their immediate question was still whether the Imperfectly Perfect Campaign was a non-profit organisation. I found myself starting to turn the tables on them. Instead of simply confirming its status, I challenged their motives and intentions as to why they wanted to know. Of course, it was merely a question, and anybody had a right to ask.

But I simply wanted to turn the tables and ask, "Why does it matter whether we're a non-profit or not?" I would respond.

"Are you looking to support a social impact movement on a global scale for change, or are you not?"

It was a straightforward question that cut to the heart of the matter. I understood that many companies were motivated by tax

ONE MAN'S MISSION TO REDEFINE IMPERFECTION

benefits regarding donations. Still, I wanted to know if they were genuinely committed to making a difference or their interest was purely transactional.

Also, anybody can do what they want here. If that is their prerogative, then so be it. I'm not here to pass judgment or claim to know why certain companies do what they do. I just knew I was out here doing my thing. If they wanted a piece of what I had built to make a difference and tap into my global network, they could come to the table and show me they had the Imperfectly Perfect Campaign's best interests at heart. After all, they were approaching, drawn in by something about the Imperfectly Perfect Campaign.

So, I made it clear that organisations that wanted to support the efforts as official sponsors for our events were more than welcome to do so. I was not interested in engaging with companies whose sole focus was on their bottom line or merely driving attention toward themselves.

Meeting a multi-millionaire mentor through a close friend of mine during this time was also a significant change for me. Their words echoed in my mind long after our conversation ended:

"If you want to make a small difference, start a non-profit. If you want to change the world on a huge scale, start a business and make sure companies pay you to be able to make that difference."

IMPERFECTLY PERFECT CAMPAIGN

This perspective turned my understanding of social impact and business on its head. The idea of creating change through entrepreneurship and leveraging commerce's power to drive meaningful impact resonated deeply with me. I saw what God was trying to show me all along.

He was showing me that the power was within me all this time to build a sustainable business model that not only fuelled my passion but also attracted support from companies eager to align with our mission and invest in me to make it happen.

I saw my 'Robin Hood' portrayal of myself coming to a reality.

The mentor's words became a guiding principle for me as I navigated the intersection of business and social good. By creating value and providing solutions to people and companies through my skillset, knowledge, and expertise, I could thrive in the process in my business and be the one to pour into my endeavours to make a difference.

It was a shift in mindset that empowered me to not only start consulting with other companies, be picked up by several international speaking bureaus and associations, delivering keynotes on my work, but also to form partnerships with companies willing to invest in my vision and through my international events.

ONE MAN'S MISSION TO REDEFINE IMPERFECTION

I no longer saw myself as playing small. I saw that true impact was not measured by the size of your organisation, but by the scale and sustainability of the change you can affect.

This sudden influx of opportunities allowed me to reassess my priorities. I no longer needed to juggle between construction jobs to keep everything moving. With each opportunity that came my way, I saw the potential to not only make the Imperfectly Perfect Campaign become sustainable but also to propel it toward even greater heights.

Whatever the opportunity put in front of me, it represented a stepping stone toward my vision of creating meaningful and lasting change in the world. What was once a distant dream had now become a reality. At the heart of my journey was the profound revelation of discovering my true self. I realised that the mission entrusted to me was not a random occurrence, but a purpose deeply ingrained within my being.

I possessed all the necessary attributes to fulfil it; I just needed a gentle reminder to awaken to this truth.

To anyone reading my story, I hope it serves as a reminder that we are all guided if we open our eyes to it. Initially, my eyes were closed, but profound changes followed once they opened. I will never claim to have all the answers to life. It would be wrong for anyone to do so because we are all on unique journeys. Where I am

IMPERFECTLY PERFECT CAMPAIGN

today, I give thanks to God. But do I have my path mapped out? No. That would mean succumbing to this world's desire to control the narrative, which does not work.

The more I took in leaps of faith, spiritual exploration, and trusting the divine, the more I could tap into my inner guidance to move forward. I urge anyone reading this to do the same. Trust that the answers are within you, and your journey, with all its unique twists and turns, leads you to where you need to be. Embrace the unknown, take leaps of faith, and consistently seek to connect with the deeper purpose that resides within you.

ONE MAN'S MISSION TO REDEFINE IMPERFECTION

EPILOGUE

To date, the Imperfectly Perfect Campaign's Global Endeavours have touched the lives of over twelve million individuals, garnering features in international media publications and networks. Supported by more than five hundred esteemed public figures spanning entertainment, sports, corporate, medical fields, personal development, faith, and spirituality, from Australia to Hollywood and beyond, the Campaign's impact continues to be nothing short of a miracle.

Founder Glenn Marsden has spearheaded an innovative global movement, going on to facilitate international events and publish two highly international best-selling book series, including a children's series titled The Magic of Imperfections, and an anthology series that unites diverse voices to reshape the dialogue surrounding mental health.

Glenn's leadership has elevated him to a revered thought leader and innovative speaker, sought after for his insights and expertise on stages worldwide.

glennmarsden.com | imperfectlyperfectcampaign.org

www.ingramcontent.com/pod-product-compliance
Lightning Source LLC
Chambersburg PA
CBHW060605080526
44585CB00013B/694